'We were
beautifully
different, and that
was okay.'

Advance Praise for WOUNDS:

"*Wounds* is a gem of writing. Daniel and Razel's styles of writing are related, but uniquely their own identities. They weave similar themes, but from their own perspectives. The writing is so raw, so real, so human."

-Mwenda Ntarangwi, PhD.
Author of *Reversed Gaze: An African Ethnography of American Anthropology*

"*Wounds* begins with Abbott and Jones writing that their pens will be their swords as they confront American racism in this time of police brutality and Black Lives Matter. And that is what Abbott and Jones do. They wield their pens against racial ignorance and injustice. But they also wield their pens toward empathy, so that we can "experience *difference* from a new perspective." *Wounds* teaches us to see the world, and race in America, in a beautiful, complex, and honest way. It asks us to bathe in how we, each, are 'beautifully different,' how 'our world is not colorless. It is colorful, and we're better for it.'"

-Sean Prentiss
Author of *Finding Abbey*

"I truly could not put the book down. Razel Jones and Daniel Abbott are speaking out boldly and bravely. They both know it is time. It is often asserted that most white folks are of good intent and only a small percentage are overtly racist. If indeed that is true, it is time for all people of good intentions to stand up for what is right. The time is now."

-Carla Roberts
President & CEO Fremont Area
Community Foundation

RAZEL JONES

&

DANIEL ABBOTT

WOUNDS

A Collaborative

Memoir in Stories

Summer Camp Publishing
PO Box 472
Banner Elk, NC 28604
SummerCampPublishing.com
Email: SummerCampPublishing@Gmail.com

This memoir is a truthful recollection of actual events in the lives of the authors. Some conversations have been recreated and/or supplemented. The names and details of some individuals have been withheld to respect their privacy.

Cover Art: Matthew Taylor Wilson
Interior Design: Brooks Rexroat for Summer Camp Publishing
Editors: Ali Braenovich and Brooks Rexroat

First Edition.
Isbn: 978-1-7353637-3-8
Library of Congress Control Number: 2020944828
Printed in the United States of America

In loving memory of Diane Cartwright, Lera Jackson, Hendrick Jones, Jr., and Bishop Robert Smith, Sr. All departed this world between July 2019 and March 2020. Thank you for your love and guidance. You have helped mold us into the men we have become, and you continue to inspire us as we follow our paths through this world without you.

Table of Contents

Foreword

RAZEL JONES

I have known esteemed novelist Daniel Abbott for more than 25 years. We met while we were both teenagers in Northern Michigan. The town we were primarily in, White Cloud, was in a rural area with a population of less than 1,200 people. While less than 10 percent of the population was comprised of African Americans, this percentage was greater than all other surrounding towns in the county combined.

Daniel is a Caucasian male who moved to the community just before beginning his high school career, and after experiencing the majority of his childhood surrounded by people of many different races on the Northeast side of Grand Rapids, Michigan. It was there that he began building deep, meaningful relationships with people from various cultures and developed a subconscious comfort with *difference*. This cultural immersion experience, in combination with his lived experience as a white male in urban, suburban, and rural communities produced an ability in him to navigate cultures dominated by whites, those dominated by blacks, and those dominated by almost every culture in-between.

In much the same way, my being an African American, born into a Caucasian-dominated geographic and social landscape forced me to learn how to navigate white-dominated cultures in order to survive. I was also fortunate to be born into a strong and proud, black family, with parents who intentionally put me in situations to affirm and celebrate being a member of black culture.

The product of both of our experiences has been the ability to seemingly seamlessly flow between black and white cultures. We both agree that this ability has ultimately been a blessing to our lives. It has produced fruitful relationships, opportunity-provoking skill-sets, and eyes and hearts awakened to the realities of racial and social disparities. We have a keen understanding of both the beauty of *difference*, and the pain of fear-based ignorance.

Later in life, Daniel and I reconnected as we happened to marry two sisters, which elevated our pre-existing friendship into a deeper level of family-ship. Previously brothers-in-experience now brothers-in-law, we have continued to observe one another's experiences of navigating racial and cultural divides, and experiencing the world through lenses of empathy with cultural sensitivity. I now am fortunate enough to be one of several black uncles to Daniel's biracial children and Daniel is the white uncle to my black daughter.

Most recently, our social media presences collided as we both responded to current reminders of race-driven inequity with stories of our experiences in Northern Michigan and beyond. These were shared after experiencing videos of the senseless murders of yet another two African Americans who did not deserve to die: Mr. Ahmaud Arbery (Date Of Birth: May 8, 1994; Date Of Death: February 23, 2020) and Mr. George Floyd (Date Of Birth: October 14, 1973; Date Of Death: May 25, 2020). May they both rest in peace, but may our peace rest until we can contribute to bringing about positive change in our country to prevent the continual adding of names to the list of women and men viciously murdered in America, primarily because of the color of their skin.

It is our hope that as we reflect on several personal stories of how the two of us have experienced the ugly head of racism in this country and what we have felt and learned based on our unique experiences, that we would expose how this mischievous, irrational monster operates. Ultimately, if we can inspire one to stand against the demonic force, this project is worth it. Furthermore, if we can provide tools—strike that—weapons…to fight, injure, and destroy the beast, then every negative experience we have encountered is worth it. Today, we urge you to challenge your comfort zone, experience *difference* from a new perspective, maximize your empathy, and see the world through another's eyes. May our pens be our swords; let the battle begin.

I'm Definitely Different

RAZEL JONES
WHITE CLOUD, MICHIGAN CIRCA 1983

When I first stepped into Mike Perrin's house, I saw the familiar and the unfamiliar. Parents, siblings, pets, food, love. All of this was also present at my house, but what was different was the way the Perrins interacted with these objects. It was the first white family's house I entered without at least one of my parents. On that visit it became clear, for the first time, that I was different. It wasn't all about racial differences. Some of it was our families had different customs. Different personalities. Different ways of doing things. Different names for things. That is the tricky part to *difference*. It's not all one thing. Everything is not about race. Yet, there are racial tendencies. Racial differences that weave in and out of the fabric of *difference* that exist between various groupings of people. On that visit, it was first clear to me.

I'm definitely different.

Memory #1: Mike had a dog.

That wasn't so strange; after all, we too had a dog. But, I can barely remember any times that our dog was inside the house. Mike slept with his dog. Our dog had his own house, outside, which is right where I liked him to be. I'm not sure that we should have had a dog, because for the most part, I don't think any of us were really dog people. Maybe my older brother, Jerome was. He seemed to be the main one to take care of our dog, Spike. I am pet-empathetic. I understand that the kind of people who should have dogs are the kind of people who don't mind a dog licking them in the face.

I was afraid of dogs. Dogs liked to jump on kids. I know it was playful, but I didn't sign up for that kind of play date. I don't speak for all black people when I say this, but I can speak for myself...I'm still not the world's biggest fan of dogs.

I have wondered if it has anything to do with racial history. Dogs haven't exactly been used in a friendly manner when it comes to African

Americans throughout American history. When a slave would escape, what animal would chase them through the woods to bring them back into subjection? It was Rover. When civil rights protestors were beaten and sprayed with fire hoses, what animal was released to attack an already subdued protestor? You got it. It was Fido and friends. Man's best friend? Perhaps. It depends what man we are talking about. Anyway, it's probably not a racial thing at all. I just don't really like dogs.

Memory #2: The Perrins ate supper. I ate dinner.

Mike and I walked from the school to the Perrin's house, about a mile away. We got to the house and entered from a side door, near the kitchen. Through an opening, we came to the living room. On a reclining chair near the wall, Mike, Sr., Mike's dad—my Uncle's childhood friend—sat quietly reading the *Times Indicator*, our local newspaper, while smoking his fragrant pipe. The new smell, like a sweet, smoky treat, filled my young nose and the living room. I liked it. It was intriguing, as I had never seen someone smoke a pipe before. Keeping straight through the living room, we came to the front door.

Stepping out the front door, we could look to the left, up the street a bit and see the 76 Service Station that Mike's dad owned. Michael, Sr. worked hard to run that business. He repaired cars, serviced vehicles, and at his gas station, you didn't have to get out of your car to get your gas. The employees would pump it for you, check your oil, and clean your windshield while you waited.

When we came back in the house, we went upstairs to the bedrooms. His youngest sister, Kim, played in her room with the door open, curious about our adventures. His older sister, Michelle, was in her room with the door shut, as teenagers do, probably hoping that our adventures wouldn't annoy her. We bypassed their rooms and made our way to the headquarters for playing throughout most of my visit—Mike's room. He had posters of athletes, mostly the Detroit Tigers. Kirk Gibson, Lance Parrish, Sweet Lou Whitaker, Jack Morris, Chet Lemon. Soon to be the 1984 World Series champions. Banners with his teams of choice, Tigers, Lakers, and Lions, I believe. The most important part of the room, at least for me, was the toys. Transformers, G.I. Joes, those little green army men, and the cars. It was like Mike had emptied the local Ben Franklin five-and-dime store of all the Hot Wheels. We played as hard as we could. As fast as we could. As much as we could. We were following the kid rules. If you want to be friends, don't make it weird—just play and play nice.

We had no conversations about race in America. Difference among the cultures. Cross cultural collaboration. No, we had conversations that felt better at the time. About Transformers. About He-Man. About Luke Sky-walker and Darth Vader. We had conversations about the WWF. Hulk Hogan. Andre the Giant. Rowdy Roddy Piper. Jesse "The Body" Ventura. Bobby "The Brain" Heenan. The Junkyard Dog.

When we grew tired of being inside, we ran out the side door to the basketball rim. He had a paved court in the backyard. It looked brand new. The hoop was probably regulation, but to my short self, it looked twelve feet high. I could tell Mike spent a lot of time out there. His shots went in more than mine, but I could dribble like a 6th grader, even though I was a 3rd grader. I didn't have a court like that at my house, so I spent most of my time dribbling my purple and yellow Lakers basketball. We played Around the World. Horse. Twenty-one, although I don't think we ever scored that many points. One-on-one—first to ten, by ones, switching to twos in the middle because it took too long.

Our play wasn't about competition. It was just about doing whatever was fun at the moment. We switched to baseball, where one person was the batter and the other was the pitcher and every other position in the infield and outfield. We were instructed by Mike's mom, Diane, not to hit the ball into any windows. We took our chances, hitting the ball through the neigh-bors' yard over near the railroad tracks that ran parallel to Mike's property.

As we went to retrieve the ball, in the distance we heard the whistle of the Chessie train headed our way. Mike knew just what to do. "Raz, do you have any coins?" I pulled out a few pennies from my lint-filled pocket and he pulled a couple from his to match. He showed me how to quickly situate the coins on the railroad tracks, as the calling whistle of the train grew louder. You could hear the cadence of the oncoming freight's moving parts. Chucka, chucka, chucka, chucka, Chucka chucka chucka chucka. We laid, almost hidden, on the ground four to five feet from the tracks near a small tree line. We could feel the Chucka, chucka, Chucka, chucka…Oncoming locomotion.

We waited for the vibrations to cease. The whistle to quiet. The caboose to fade into the distance. It was time to collect our bounty. We gathered the disfigured coins that were flattened between the rails and the train. The force of the rails was strong enough to manipulate the copper. You couldn't even tell it was a penny anymore. You could smell the dust released by the heat of the impact.

Mike became very serious, his blue eyes expanding in alarm. "Raz, don't tell my parents we were by the railroad tracks." He said it so seriously, it became obvious that he was previously warned not to conduct the metamorphic experiment again. We weren't supposed to put those coins on the tracks. It was dangerous for two boys our age to be that close to an approaching train. It was also illegal to mutilate and disfigure money like we had just done. I had wondered why we were lying down hiding after setting our penny traps. We went back to playing in Mike's yard. In the middle of our adventure, only about two hours in, although it felt like more, Mike's mom called from the kitchen, "Michael, it's time for supper."

I listened void of understanding...Mike kept playing, so I kept playing. I had no idea what supper was all about. Was it a chore? Was it a religious ritual? Was it a nice way of saying something like using the bathroom? I really had no idea. But, judging from the fact that Mike kept playing, I thought, this supper thing must not be too important.

Mike's mom had insisted I call her Diane, rather than Mrs. Perrin. I wasn't so sure about that considering my dad had told me to always refer to adults as Mr. and Mrs. A few minutes later, Diane called out to Mike again. This time with a different tone than the first time. This was the day I discovered Mike's full name: "Michael. Arthur. Perrin!"

This expansion of his name got Mike's attention. Mike replied in a way that was a guarantee of a smack in the mouth, a thump on the head, a swat on the rear, or, at least the loss of any privilege possible for a long, long time. He said it...He responded with the word forbidden by black parents throughout the generations...And he yelled it when he replied, "WHAT?" I knew his life was in jeopardy. If that was me, responding with a "WHAT!" the locomotion of my father, Hank Jones would have been approaching at full force...Chucka, Chucka, Chucka, Chucka...I just knew that my visit would soon end. No more pennies on the railroad tracks for me. His sentence would soon commence.

Instead, she finished her thought, "I told you it's supper time. Now you guys come eat."

Wait…that was it? No violence? No threats? At that moment I had multiple, concurrent revelations of our differences. Supper was the same thing as dinner. They eat supper, and they eat it way earlier than we eat dinner. We weren't being watched very closely. In fact, although I didn't know I was being a criminal, we had just gotten away with breaking the law by the railroad tracks. Mike didn't get threatened when he ignored his mom. Mike didn't get knocked down when he answered, "What?" His interactions with authority seemed different than mine.

I remember Diane, over the years, remarking about how respectful I was. I was full of thank-yous, yes ma'ams, pleases, and may Is. I was concerned about how I was perceived. I was concerned about representing my family. Representing my race. I was concerned about following the rules. That day, Mike led me on an expedition of fun. Mike was full of…Adventure. Exploration. Curiosity. Where I worried, he leaped. Where I hesitated, he plunged. Where I thought, he acted. When I obeyed, he questioned.

Mike and I were the same in what we liked to play with. What we liked to watch on television. Where we went to school. Our parents even went to school together. We were from the same community. We were probably even born at the same hospital. But, even with all of those commonalities, we lived very different lives with very different experiences. Our traditions were not the same. Our standards of conduct were not the same. Our personalities were not the same. What we ate was not the same. The music we listened to at home was not the same. Our pets were not the same. Our family's dynamics were not the same. The way we referred to and interacted with adults was not the same. Our perceptions were not the same. Our lives were not the same. We could debate which parts were applicable to race, which to family differences, which to personality and style, but there is no debate that we were different.

We were beautifully different, and that was okay. This is the lesson I long for so many people to realize. For every person who feels like they're saying something fantastic to me when they state that they're "colorblind." Don't be colorblind. What is the joy in choosing to miss out on all of the beauty that comes with the richness of color and hue and diversity that God created to purposely exist in this Earth? The notion that some feel it a good thing to be colorblind is in error. What's wrong with *difference*?

I understand the intent of the statement, but here's what you're missing if you buy in to this concept of colorblindness. The sentiment that you should see no color suggests that there is something wrong with my color. With my *difference*. My color is beautiful. Your color is beautiful. Why can't we be different and beautiful? Why do I have to be just like you to be considered good? Our world is not colorless. It is colorful, and we're better for it.

You are perfectly pigmented. It is not your color that defines who you are. Your color just animates you. Like the choosing of which color to use when kids pull from the Crayola sixty-four pack, our color was simply the selection God made to bring His picture to life. Animation. What defines you is your character. You are the character. What do you do? How do you interact with creation? What decisions do you make? What comes out of your mouth? What is your role? Character. If there is a part of any of us that needs adjusting, that needs development, it is not the color. Not the animation. It is the character. Develop your character.

Commonalities? We have plenty. Differences? We have plenty of those too. There are ways that any two of us are the same. There are ways that any two of us are different. This is the beauty of connection. We all have the potential for synergies in our areas of *sameness*. We all have the potential for complementary partnerships in our areas of *difference*. We need both. Let me be different. Let me be great. For those of you who think that there is some rectitude in us all being identical, robotic beings, I definitely disagree. It is not our differences that separate us. It is the denial of the beauty and rightness of those differences that separates us.

The "N" Word

DANIEL ABBOTT
NEWAYGO, MICHIGAN 1991

Back then my head was swimming with hoop dreams. A bald rubber Spalding weaving between my legs, echoing off the concrete. I wore baggy Nike shorts and too-big t-shirts. All-white tube socks and black Nike Dopemans. My shoe had a hole in the right toe from dragging my foot on layups. These days they'd call it swag; back then my dad called it a waste of money.

I was, I am, a different kind of dude.

I grew up on the Northeast side of Grand Rapids, Michigan with working-class parents. We lived on the edge of urban and suburban, in Hidden Valley apartments, with a mosaic of transitional families. A neighborhood where different was normal. A place where I could be different, but also belong. My friends were white and black and brown. Our parents all seemed to be struggling toward something better: a college degree, a higher paying job, an opportunity. Some other, better life on the horizon.

I enjoyed being a kid at Hidden Valley. We played Super Mario Bros and Tetris and Tecmo Bowl in each other's basements. We played touch football in the street and scraped our elbows and knees. Or we'd pack a cooler and ball all day on the complex's asphalt court, our fingers stained black, the nets aged gray. Dawn to dusk. Even at a young age I believed in the religion of Alarm Clock. I believed in hard work. That life was without limits if you were willing to suffer to achieve.

My family moved to Grand Rapids when I was in 1st grade. When my dad took a job in the city and didn't want to make the forty-five-minute commute south from a small town called Newaygo. We'd moved for the convenience. My parents had roots in the Newaygo area. Their friends were there. Their family was there. Newaygo was their home. Grand Rapids was mine. When my parents told me we were moving back north the summer before my freshman year of high school, I cried.

I knew Newaygo. We often made that trip up M-37 to visit my grand-parents on Sundays. I was born ten miles away at Gerber Hospital in Fre-mont, just a year and a few weeks after Razel. There was no mall in Newaygo. No movie theater. There wasn't even a McDonalds at the time. Newaygo was too slow for a city slicker like me. It felt leagues away from my comfort zone, from my friends, from the opportunity to showcase my skills on the basketball court, to fulfill my dream of a Division I scholarship and beyond. At fourteen, the move north felt tragic.

I was just a little fella when I started my freshman year of high school. Five-foot-three and a buck fifteen. Suddenly shy. I'd always been a little so-cially awkward, but in Newaygo I felt socially inept. In Newaygo different felt different. There I was definitely different. Defiantly different. The small-town vibe just didn't jibe with how I moved through the world. The concrete in the city had a music to it. A cadence on par with my pulse. The cement in Newaygo had no sound. The place was quiet. No rhythm. No soul. It didn't have a voice that spoke to me. I didn't appreciate nature back then. I didn't value the beauty of that small town built on the banks of the Muskegon river. Surrounded by lakes rich with walleye, pike, bluegill, and bass. The op-portunities to explore the woods and the riverbank. That was before I loved to fish and kayak and hike. Back then I hooped. They didn't hoop in Newaygo, they played basketball. And if you don't know the difference, buckle up—this book is going to be a bumpy ride.

Newaygo was, and still is, racially homogenous. Impeccably white. A place you often see Confederate flags and Make America Great Again bumper stickers pasted side-by-side on Chevys and Dodges and Fords. A thriving population of #AllLivesMatter types. Life is good in Newaygo and they don't want it to change. They are threatened by change. The problems of the country, city problems, diversity problems: those are not Newaygo problems. Like many racially homogenous white towns, a large percentage of the Americans living in Newaygo like to pretend the country isn't broken, isn't a steaming pile of inequality, because it isn't. Not to them. To them there is harmony.

But what happens when that harmony is disrupted? When a black or brown face moves into their sphere of comfort. Or a white kid from the city with a basketball weaving between his legs while he walks. I brought Grand Rapids with me to Newaygo. I brought *difference*. I was used to a fluid concept of harmony. I was used to diversity. Homogenous harmony has walls. As a fourteen-year-old boy in Newaygo, I felt those walls.

I believe in harmony without walls. In fluidity. I know people in Newaygo who share my sentiments. But most of those people choose silence. They were silent when I moved there in the early 90s. Most of them are silent now. As a fourteen-year-old boy, what was loudest about that racially homogenous small town was that *difference* was not welcome. In Newaygo I didn't belong.

The year I moved to Newaygo there was a group of kids claiming to support the Third Reich. Third Reich: Nazi infamy. White supremacy. Those kids were poseurs, for sure. Punks, absolutely. Hormonal teenagers with rebellious bones. The children of parents with archaic ideologies. Ideologies that have no place in a civilized world. I think about them now and I cringe. I pity them. At age fourteen though, they scared me. Hearing the "N" word tossed around in casual conversation wasn't something I was accustomed to. That wasn't how I was raised. It wasn't a word used, not by anyone in my household, not by the people in my circles who had white skin.

About a month into the school year two of my friends from Grand Rapids, Larry and Matt, came to visit for the weekend. Larry was black and Matt was half-Korean, half-white. We'd known each other since elementary school. Spent countless nights at each other's houses. Larry's stepdad Don and Matt's stepdad Jim were friends with my dad.

We spent that weekend hooping in my driveway and exploring downtown Newaygo. We didn't cause trouble. Didn't do anything crazy. We popped our heads in stores, walked around like teenage boys do, dribbling basketballs, checking out girls. We were high off the invincibility of youth. We owned the space we occupied. I wonder now what the people in small town Newaygo saw that weekend. What words were whispered? What was discussed at their dinner tables? Did me being with my black friend Larry settle some argument about me? Did that make up their minds about the kid from Grand Rapids who dressed different, talked different, moved different? Did they come to some conclusion about the kid whose haircut was different, fashioned after my favorite black basketball players, clipper-cut low and bald on the sides, blended as best as I could do myself, leaning over the bathroom sink with a hand mirror, the rattling sound of some old rusty Wahls?

I don't know. I was oblivious to racism back then. My eyes weren't open like they are now. If we got any looks, I'd probably assumed they were the looks we got in the city, the looks all kids got when they wandered out into the world alone. Where are your parents? Those, I'm watching you looks: you better not be stealing. You better not start any trouble. You better not be up to no good. I know now that day in Newaygo, Larry, Matt, and I were being watched by at least one.

On Monday one of the Third Reich kids approached me. I remember him. I remember his name, but I won't name him here. I pray he knows the difference between meek and weak and that my moral compass takes precedence over my righteous indignation. I'd like to think it does. I'd like to think I could see this boy as a man and look him in the eyes, speak to him, remind him of that moment twenty-eight years ago and allow him the opportunity to apologize. But most of all I pray that the Third Reich kid has changed. I pray that Third Reich kid has grown into a man much different than the boy he was.

"So who was that shadow following you around this weekend?" The Third Reich boy asked me that Monday at my locker.

When I think back to that moment, I imagine the Third Reich boy the weekend before, leering, looming. My friends and I had swagger. That hateful boy didn't have the confidence we had. The invincibility. He knew he was mortal. The way he watched us. The way he followed us. He was the real shadow that day, lurking.

That day at my locker I still believed I was a citizen of one America. I believed I was a part of that America. I now know that I am not. I now know I am *other*. That day I looked at the Third Reich boy and I raised an eyebrow. I had no idea what he was talking about, but I didn't like his tone. I didn't like the smirk on his pimply face. The violence in his gate. His clenched fists. He wasn't much bigger than I was, but he had this power I still don't fully understand. The power of numbers. He was by himself, but he wasn't alone. I was. More alone than alone. On an island inside of an island. I was prey.

"Huh?" was all I could muster. I hate that me. The real me would've reacted differently. The real me would've stood his ground. That me, that fourteen-year-old me, that five-foot-three and a buck-fifteen me, that fresh-man-year-at-Newaygo-High-School me was scared. That me was underdeveloped in size and understanding. In maturity. That me had his own bubble mentality. In my bubble there was black culture. There was hip-hop music. The music of the concrete. My bubble was burst that day in Newaygo. The beginning of my cultural awareness was born.

"That nigger." He said it like the word gave him pleasure. A drink of cold water on a humid day. A Thanksgiving nap. A hotel bed after a long day on the road. Then he was gone. A coward. Like a person afraid of a small animal. He left me standing at my locker. The Grand Rapids me would have thrown a punch. I'd never been one to suffer bullies. I'd been suspended in middle school countless times for fighting and almost always in defense of someone being picked on. But I was a long way from Grand Rapids. The Newaygo me stood at his locker and did nothing.

I knew trouble was coming. That's how it felt. Like discussions had been had. Plans had been made. Physically I was like them. I was white, like them. My parents were white, like their parents. But I knew my skin would not keep me safe in that place. I was guilty by association. Guilty because of my black friend Larry. I am still guilty by association. By my marriage to my black wife, Vanessa. By my eight biracial children.

That weekend in Newaygo, I was discovered. I remain discovered. Stand before you discovered. I was different. I am different. I was definitely different.

I'm definitely different.

After that day I was called nigger lover. White nigger. Wigger. A group of seniors took a particular interest in me. They'd leave their government class with their newspapers rolled up and hit me across the back of my head. "Nigger lover. White nigger. Wigger." They liked to circle me and shove me back and forth. Corner me in the bathroom, force me into a stall, shove my head into the toilet.

Distrust. Fear. Rage. Confusion.

Wasn't I white like they were? Wasn't I the same? I know now that I wasn't. That I'd always been different. But at the time, different felt scary. Different meant naked. Exposed. Newaygo created me. A me that took years to tame. A me with open eyes and clenched fists. A me that would grow nine inches in two years. A me that would be swallowed by the seed they planted. A violent me. A me I'm not proud of. But a necessary me. A me who needed to emerge in order to survive.

At fourteen my experience with the Third Reich boy had given me a glimpse of what it means to be black in America. Just a glimpse. It was enough to make me want to shield my eyes. To look at life through the creases of my fingers. That year helped prepare me to father biracial children. That year led me to understand the difference, the obstacles that black people face in America. In that way, my freshman year at Newaygo High School was a gift. So for now I thank you, Third Reich boy. I don't know if I'm ready to see you though. I don't know if I'm emotionally mature enough to see you. Have enough self-control to see you.

You created in me a fear. A fear that led to anger. An anger that led to violence. A vice. A vice that I have conquered. I believe I have conquered. I hope I have conquered.

Third Reich boy: I'm no longer looking at the country you cling to between the creases of my fingers. My chin is tucked. My chest is out. My shoulders are pinned back. My eyes are wide. Thank you, Third Reich boy for allowing me to see. I'm better for the experience. I don't want to hurt you; I want you to listen. I don't want to punish you; I want you to think. I believe in justice, not revenge. I want to believe, if I ever see you again, I won't hurt you. But if I'm being honest, I really don't know.

Because I'm wounded. A wounded man is a dangerous man.

And man, oh man, do I have wounds.

Different is Lonely

RAZEL JONES
WHITE CLOUD, MICHIGAN 1985

Entering the new year, 1985. Another normally abnormal, treacherous Michigan winter was coming to an end. I was nine years old. Back then, my sport of choice was basketball. My team was the Lakers. Showtime. Magic Johnson on the fast break with the no-look pass. James Worthy elevating for the statue of liberty dunk. Michael Cooper and Jamaal "Silk" Wilkes draining those long-range threes. Byron Scott feeding the rock to Kareem, who liked to turn and release that signature, undefendable sky hook. The Lake Show captivated my attention and caused me to love the game.

This captivation was shared by friends at school who were also fans of the Lakers. In baseball, there was generally loyalty to the Tigers; in football, many held a painful allegiance to the ever-disappointing Lions (although I was a Cowboys fan as long as I can remember); in basketball some had split support to the Pistons and the Lakers, but for me it was all about the Lakers. Maybe it was the fact that the central character on the Lakers was Earvin "Magic" Johnson—a true Michigander from Lansing, just under two hours away. The former star of the Michigan State Spartans made Michigan more famous. Michigan bred—and not from Detroit. It was nice to see that Michigan had something to offer in addition to Detroit. It also didn't hurt that the Lakers knew how to win, with five championships in the 1980s alone.

Every day at recess, we played basketball, imagining we were the world champs. We couldn't wait for recess. So many of my good childhood memories in White Cloud were made during recess. I had some good times, but I had some incredibly rough times as well.

White Cloud was not heavily populated with black people. Most of the people I experienced on a daily basis did not look like me. I never had a black teacher in White Cloud. Never. In fact, it wasn't until my third year of college that I experienced a black teacher. Never a black administrator either. In those elementary years, barely any other black students in my classes. Different is lonely.

At the time, I assumed my experiences matriculating through that school, through that community, were normal. I had nothing to compare it to. Now, after having broader experiences, after learning others' experiences, I know it was not normal. Indeed, it was abnormal.

Abnormal. From the day I first entered the halls of Jack D. Jones Elementary School for my first half-day of kindergarten. My face, along with Aisha Shelmon's, were the only faces of color in a grade of around fifty. Aisha was somewhat familiar. Our families were connected, as most black families in White Cloud were. We attended the same church. My godmother was her aunt. I didn't know Aisha well, but I knew her. It was nice to see someone I knew in that room of newness. In hindsight, it was nice to see someone else who was black in that room of whiteness. Each new student was experiencing newness. Only two of us though, were experiencing *difference*. I moved throughout the days excited, yet nervous about making friends and sharing experiences. What I wasn't nervous about was having fun. Having fun was what would get me through this laborious journey.

Four years later, I played on the elementary school basketball courts with Brent, Mike, Bill, and other white kids, as we imitated mostly black basketball stars who we idolized. I was the only one who had brown skin. That prop of pigment made me more accurately reflect the skin of the heroes we were enamored by. The Lakers weren't our only subjects. We mostly mimicked the not-so-distant high school players who performed their enchantment just down the hill, the pine hill, which led to the back door of the varsity basketball locker room in the high school gym.

The team was mostly comprised of big white boys who appeared as men to us pre-pubescents. Giants to us. Bill Stoskoff, Duane Gibson, Matt Wilks; they all towered above our elementary-sized frames. Then, there was probably the quickest athlete I had ever seen in White Cloud. He was so fast. A brother in the melanin-infused sense of the word, Troy Snell. We were fans of all those guys, for sure...but, when it came time to select which player we would try to be like on that playground court, the one we all wanted to be was Gerald Stewart.

He was a black teenager, but he seemed like a man to us. He had swag on and off the court. Gerald was a natural leader. He was seemingly liked by all. Blue jean jackets, multicolored tops, designer sweaters with the collared shirts underneath, fresh Air Force Ones, way back when Nelly was a little fella, like I was then. Run DMC bringing the noise as the boombox was carried on the shoulders of rural teenagers recreating an urban experience. Before Run told us about his Adidas, Gerald rocked the swoosh. Close-cut, waves and a tapered fade. Gerald was the man.

He was faster than his opponents. Known for no-look passes, reminiscent of Magic. A silky jumper, effortlessly released. His coffee brown fingers rolled beautifully off the burnt-sienna orangish, brownish ball. Spalding rotation. Hold the follow-through for effect. In synchrony. In harmony. In the net. An average-sized shooting guard, but he could jump out the gym. Known to cross-over a defender and throw down a dunk on the fast break, sending the crowd—especially, the upper elementary emulators we had all become—into a frenzied uproar.

When the recess bell blasted to alert us of our thirty minutes of freedom and escape, we would enter stage right. Take our positions. Pick our teams. Select our roles. I perpetually auditioned for the role of Gerald, but there was no guarantee. There were days my white co-stars: Brent, Mike, or Bill would beat me to it. They may not have looked the part as naturally as I did, but they wanted the role just as badly.

The fact that Brent was imitating a black guy in front of all of our class meant everything. Brent was the most popular white kid in the school at the time. Athletic. Smart. The girls liked him. He was a little taller than the rest of us. A little more athletic than the rest of us. He seemed to mature faster than the rest of us. The rest of the class would catch up to him in height later. The older we got, the more equal we became. Brent and I had the kind of friendship most kids don't get to experience.

His father once pulled my dad out of a wrecked car, probably saving his life. His mother grew up in close proximity to my parents and my older cousins on my mom's side, the Dukes. His mother Cindy always treated me with love. Food. Conversation. I was welcome in her home. Our families were connected. Brent and I were another generationally-connected friendship.

I remember in 5th grade a teacher affirming me and Brent's friendship. His name was Mr. Brewster, an older white man who loved Beethoven and British Literature. The tallest teacher I had ever seen. The tallest *man* I had ever seen. He seemed like he was seven-feet-tall back then. He was more like six-five though. A gentle, intellectual giant. He pulled us aside one day. No doubt seeing the purity of our cross-cultural friendship, he implored us to cherish and protect what we had. I knew it was connected to race, but to 5th-grade me, it wasn't such a big deal. We didn't care about that. We just wanted to have fun. To play our sports. To play as much as we could—as hard as we could.

Brent and I ended up being college roommates our freshmen year at Grand Valley State University. Brent studied business-human resources and ended up in education. I studied English education, and ended up in human resources. He is now the principal of White Cloud High School. I'm glad he's there. I'm glad our connection mattered.

On the playground basketball courts, Brent, the most popular kid in school, imitated Gerald Stewart, a black kid we looked up to. For those thirty minutes of the day, it felt okay to be black in White Cloud. Powerful to be black. Acceptable to be black. It was cool to be black.

It was cool for that half hour.

It wasn't as cool at other times. I recall the year prior when I built up the confidence to hand a note to little, cute, white Jessica, who I had known since those early kindergarten days. I knew she thought I was cool. We laughed a lot. We had fun. So, the shy black kid—the only black boy, at the time—skipped the playground theatrics on the lower elementary basketball court that particular day. My friends would have to play without me. My adventure and assignment that day was to pursue my crush.

Nine-year-old me was a little chubby, in spite of the constant basketball. Like Arnold, from *Different Strokes*. Like Emmanuel Lewis, in *Webster,* I was just a little shorter than most of the class, and had a round face with slightly bulging cheeks, which made me the victim of many uncomfortable cheek squeezes. Nine-year-old me had begun to believe the frequented chorus, "He's so cute..." that rang from adults and peers. For whatever reason, white people liked to touch my hair, as if it wasn't actually attached to my head. It was like we were at an exotic petting zoo, and I was the main attraction. Invaded. I didn't really like it, but didn't have the skills to stop it. Even then, realizing that I had to remain approachable. Safe. Later in life, I would learn to resist the squeezes of my cheeks and the pats of my head. I escaped the zoo.

So, I continued my mission. Operation, find Jessica. Deliver the package—a carefully folded note written on paper from my Trapper Keeper with the frayed edges still dangling. Three folds: one in half the long way, then one down, and another. I had tucked in the fray, decorated the hopeful contract, and was searching for Jessica on the playground. Looking for the right time to give her my proposal.

When I saw her I didn't hesitate, otherwise I would've never gone through with it. I approached her in the same manner I would approach the quarterback in our touch football games after a five-second count. One Mississippi. Two Mississippi. Three Mississippi. Four Mississippi. Five Mississippi. Rush!

I tossed the note at her as she played hopscotch with other girls beneath the covered area just outside the side doors of the school, leading to the playground. As covertly as I could, which was not stealth or smooth at all, I tossed the note. The quick release of the note was the typical exchange between a preteen girl and boy. A boy who had not yet acknowledged to his family that he liked girls. A boy who preferred to keep them thinking he believed girls to be yucky and boring. I wanted to look back to see her reaction, but I couldn't. It was too risky. What if she rejected my request? What if she disliked my idea? I wanted to know her answer, but I didn't want her answer to be no.

The note gave her the option to check *Yes, No,* or *Maybe,* with my most creative drawing of hearts, stars, and things I believed girls like Jessica liked. The innocent proposal, intended to propel interest to whatever came after interest. I didn't know. How could I have known? I had never taken that step.

"Will you go out with me?" No thought was given to where we would go. How we'd get there. We really couldn't go anywhere. That's just how we 3rd graders described our idea of relationships. I ran with all my might, not looking back to see what her reaction to the heart I had poured on that page would be.

Awaiting the response, I was freed to return to the normal boyhood activities. Maybe it was more basketball, football, tetherball, monkey-in-the middle. I don't remember, but whatever it was had surely been decided for me that day as I was absent for the brainstorming session.

Time moved slowly that day. What would she say? Why was it taking so long to hear a response? In my head, she would come pull me aside during that same recess and accept the manifesto, and we would then hold hands for a minute or something, before I would get back to my boys. Instead, the day ended. To our buses we marched. Still with no response to my invitation. Not a word. Maybe she wasn't interested. Maybe she didn't like the hearts. I wasn't great at drawing stars. It was probably the stars. Was it too much? Would she ever talk to me again? Would she ever laugh with me again?

I didn't see Jessica the next morning, since she was in a different homeroom class. I'd have to wait until recess to find her. She'd probably be near the hopscotch squares painted on the cement, an oasis that drew the girl groups from our 3rd grade class.

When the recess bell echoed I came out the door to the playground. There was instant nervousness as I saw her approaching. She looked nervous too. Her eyes were wide. She was surrounded by a few other girls who had likely been her sounding board. She was closer in her approach, attempting to avoid the stampede of boys and girls anxious to capitalize on the full-time allotment of recess. I was frozen. It was like she'd been out there in position before the bell had ever rung.

She spotted me and handed the letter back to me. I could tell the territory had already been explored. It had been considered. I just knew she had opened it and read every word, made her selection, carefully refolded, and safeguarded the package until she would have the opportunity to return it to me with an answer. I opened it: no mark anywhere.

"I asked my mom if I could check yes and she told me I couldn't." Some explanation followed about the obvious fact that I was black and she was white. I knew this all too well. I lived it everyday, but my youthful mind hadn't decided that it mattered. Some adult mind had. Even though I was only a child, I knew I was definitely different.

I shrugged. Attempted to play it cool. Acknowledged. Moved on physically. Physically. My blackness. My *otherness*. My colorfulness had blocked my opportunity. I did a scan of the playground to find my next place of escape and went back to being someone else. Maybe I wouldn't try to be Gerald today. How about Matt Wilks? He had a nice jumper. He didn't have to deal with being black. At that moment, it wasn't cool to be me. It wasn't cool to be black.

The half hour ended. The bell rang again. It was time to return to class.

Mentally and emotionally, I'm still moving on. Not because I was desperate to be in a relationship with Jessica. I didn't even know what a relationship really was. Instead, because she wanted to check yes but she was instructed to check no. In defiance of her mom, and I want to believe out of respect for me, she checked nothing at all. She did do what most adults still don't have the courage to do. She had a conversation with me about her feelings. She wanted to protect the friendship we had. She wanted to be able to keep on laughing. To keep playing. She did think I was cool. She was pretty cool too.

Handcuffs

DANIEL ABBOTT
NEWAYGO, MICHIGAN 1994

I met Stevie Thomas at a basketball tournament in Kent City, Michigan when we were both fifteen. He was black and from Chicago. Another concrete kid like I was. His mouth was a circus back then. Always telling jokes and sometimes lies. I know now that was Stevie's way of dealing with trauma: The loss of his father at age thirteen. The loss of a close uncle a month later. Stevie's coping mechanism was laughter. Distraction and misdirection. His way of pretending his way through a life that had dealt him a bad hand.

Stevie's mouth and my mind made a good marriage. I wasn't bothered by his innocent lies. I liked being around him. His nonstop chatter allowed me to slip into my own persona. Around Stevie, I became the quiet white boy in the hoodie, leaning against a wall, watching the room with a basketball tucked in his arm. Around Stevie I was allowed to hide. Behind his mouth. Behind blackness. Behind ball.

When Stevie was ten, he had been dragged kicking and screaming to White Cloud, a town nine miles north of Newaygo. The Cloud had a small population of black people. Some born and raised there and some were city immigrants like me and Stevie. Shortly after that tournament in Kent City I started spending time in White Cloud. I discovered my place around Stevie and other black kids there. I feigned solace. Internally I dealt with the emotions of being wrecked by Newaygo.

Besides a little diversity, what made The Cloud different than Newaygo was the Mill Pond. That place became my weekend and summertime refuge. We hooped at the Mill Pond. The basketball court was a small slab of urban. Double rims and cracked cement. There was no key and no lines. Often there were no nets—we had to buy our own. Someone would back their car onto the court and we'd stand on the hood or the trunk, and weave the net through the rim's eyelets.

The Mill Pond reminded me of courts in Grand Rapids. The trash talk. The fights. Families in The Cloud had beef. That beef seemed to always find its way to the court. Hands were thrown. The occasional pistol was popped. The police would park and watch, looking for someone slipping, someone with warrants. They'd sit and wait until they got bored, hoping to take someone off to jail, though in all my time in White Cloud I don't recall anyone ever leaving the Mill Pond in handcuffs.

Stevie's house was my home base when I came to The Cloud. His mother Yvette always treated me with love. Food. Conversation. I was welcome in her home. With her boyfriend Melvin it was hit or miss, depending on his mood. Melvin put the "P" in personality. He had swagger. He had slang. He was Chicago. Chicago trapped in White Cloud. "Shawty Shawty, Mayne. Jackball, Mayne." Always with his smirk. Always working some kind of angle. Always trying to get over. Most of the time, Melvin showed me the same love as Yvette. Some days, though, he'd be in a mood. Those days, he found a reason to kick me out the house. I wonder now if it was racial. If he brought baggage from Chicago to The Cloud. If his justified frustration of being black in a white world caused him to bring vengeance upon me because of my skin. I don't know.

Nights Melvin kicked me out, Stevie always left with me, and our destination was always the same. We'd make our way up Tulip Street to his Aunt Diane's house for a meal and a couch. She always gave us both. Never gave us grief. It didn't matter what time of night it was, Diane always let us in the door. She'd chain smoke her Newports and shake her head when we told her about Melvin. She'd allow us access to the deep freezer on her back porch where we'd usually find the frozen Schwan's Man's pizzas we'd devour until we were full. Then we'd be back in the freezer later that night, looking to devour some more.

Sometimes we'd sit at a black marble coffee table and play spades. Diane Cartwright had a loud bark and soft eyes. Loving eyes. Pitying eyes. Eyes that had seen everything life had to offer and she wasn't impressed. Had taken every blow that hardship had thrown and was still standing. Her trailer was old. Rotten. It smelled like mildew and cigarettes. No candles or incense, just the occasional smell of bleach from what was left of the linoleum peeling off the kitchen floor. The carpet was more dirt than fiber. Plastic stapled over the windows to trap the heat in winter and keep the flies out in summer.

The most prized décor: photographs of her children covering the walls. Her home was a shelter for a squad of knuckleheads like me. I wasn't special, yet somehow she made me feel special. I was wanted. If only for a night. I was wanted.

I'd survived two-and-a-half years at Newaygo High School. By my junior year, the insults had quieted down. At least to my face. There were no more rolled-up newspapers across the back of my head. The seniors from that government class my freshman year had all moved on. I survived Newaygo. I survived. I just had to make it to the weekend so I could hang out with Stevie in The Cloud. Make it to the Mill Pond. Make it to basketball season. Make it from the end of basketball season to summer. Check points.

A line between white and black had been drawn in my life. I straddled that line with an ache I had no name for. An ache I now understand as identity crisis. White people in Newaygo thought I wanted to be black. I didn't. I was me. I'd always been me. As a teen I just didn't know what me meant. Around Stevie and his black friends I was accepted. Back then I believed my acceptance was conditional. My city roots. My swagger on the court. The way I seemingly seamlessly assimilated to black culture. Accepted because I checked my whiteness at the door. Because I embraced being the white boy.

After closer examination, I believe I was wrong. Black kids in The Cloud grew up around other white boys. They grew up in rural white America. They grew up within walls. Naturally, those black boys created their own circle within those walls. A circle that was off-limits to most of those White Cloud white boys rooted in that small-town culture. I was accepted into their circle because I balled like they balled. Because we listened to the same music. Because I had experienced discrimination of my own, of course not on the same level that a black boy had experienced, but what made me different than those small-town white boys is that I knew. I acknowledged the presence of that white world. I was what they now call woke.

Back then I was offended by the way my black friends *white boy'd* me. I was cool, for a white boy. I had handles, for a white boy. Hops, for a white boy. Rhythm, for a white boy. I could rap, for a white boy. I'd been rejected by white people and embraced by black people. As a teenager I felt misunderstood. I felt confused. Somewhere in that confusion was me. The me I was destined to become.

As an adult I spent years wrestling with my identity. What my experiences in Newaygo County created. Why even at a young age I was drawn to black culture. Run DMC and Easy E and NWA. Before hip hop evolved into Biggie, Pac, and Nas. The Roots, Mos Def, and Talib Kweli. Why I married black. Why I've loved black. Was it because at a young age one of my best friends was black? I spent a lot of time with Larry's family when I was a child in Grand Rapids. I had separate and equal and silent crushes on his older sister, Stephanie and his younger sister, Melissa. Or was it sports? My heroes were black. I'd spent an entire summer trying to perfect Isaiah Thomas' baseline on-the-run fading out of bounds jumper. Tim Hardaway's Killer Crossover. MJ's every move.

As a child in Grand Rapids I didn't feel different. Like any kid, I embraced what I enjoyed. I felt comfortable around Larry and his family. I felt comfortable around the other black kids in my neighborhood, the Hispanic kids, the white kids. *Difference* wasn't different; it was normal. After Newaygo, after White Cloud, I began to resent the labels. I began to resent being misunderstood. In time I came to a simple and divine conclusion. I was meant to walk my path. I was built to walk my path. I was meant to be a white man immersed in black culture. I was, I am, just a different kind of dude.

Back then and even now, my black friends and family members often tell me they don't consider me white. I don't think that's what they really mean. What they mean is they feel safe with me. They mean they love me and feel loved in return. They don't fear the noose in my presence. Their face being pressed against the concrete. My knee pressed against their neck. My weight bearing down. When they say they don't consider me white, what they mean is that I see them. That I'm with them. That I won't stand for the little white genocides they're subjected to one podium speech at a time.

I am blessed to have lived a life of diversity, but make no mistake: I am white. Physically and legally. But my whiteness does not define me. Who I am is a husband, a father, and a writer. Those are the aspects of me I am proud of. I am not proud of my heritage. My ancestors are a burden. Allow me that burden. Of the sins I didn't commit. Allow me the apology you'll never receive. Allow my life to be an example of hope. Of love. Allow this book to be my action, my strength, my voice. Grant me permission to be accountable.

Accountability is the only real beginning to change.

By my junior year at Newaygo High School my body had grown. My gait had changed. The bullying had stopped. Mornings before school I'd play basketball in the gym. And here I'll admit: my shy, white boy persona—when I stepped out of the hoodie and onto the court—that guy was gone. I was nasty back then. I was mean. I flipped it on them. I'd become the bully. It was beyond a desire to win; my aim was to destroy. I took pleasure in narrating the destruction. Talking to you, telling you what I was going to do and doing it. I had that Mamba Mentality. Kobe. Rest in peace, Kobe.

One of those Newaygo gym mornings I was playing someone one-on-one to fifty. Ones and twos, deuce game, make it take it. The kid hit a two from the top of the key and had the audacity to smile at me. The audacity. When he missed his next shot and I snatched the rebound, I went back to the top of the key. Flick. Swish. "2-2," I told him. "I bet you don't score again."

He smiled. I wasn't smiling.

Flick. Swish. "4-2," I told him. "Bet fifty push-ups you won't score again."

I smiled. He wasn't smiling.

Flick. Swish.

Flick. Swish. "8-2," I told him. "You're kinda quiet," I said.

At 26-2 he stopped playing defense. At 40-2 he tried to quit, but I chastised him. I don't recall the words, but I imagine it had something to do with his masculinity. It was the 90s, when there was no greater insult than calling a male the equivalent of a female dog. I went on to make 25 consecutive shots from behind the arc. Not my personal best, but definitely my personal best in an actual game. I was a jerk. I'd never behave that way now. Looking back, I think that simmering anger was begging to be released. I think I wanted to fight. Wanted an excuse to fight. My junior year at Newaygo that excuse was provided.

It was the morning of an assembly. I don't remember what the assembly was about, but I know it was during basketball season. My last basketball season at Newaygo. The day started like most days did, with a pickup game, and like most days, I was breaking ankles and running my mouth. Looking back, I think that was a defense mechanism. I think basketball was my power. It was my place of confidence. My response to the bullying I experienced my freshman year. The court was the space I owned in the world. I don't remember the moments leading up to the words that were said. The words that changed the course of my life. But I'm sure I'm not blameless. I'm sure I was the one doing the bullying that morning, in my own way.

The kid wasn't a hooper. He wasn't even a basketball player. He wore tight jeans at a time it wasn't cool to wear tight jeans. He wore combat boots that clunked against the gym floor. I'm sure I destroyed him. I'm sure I humiliated him. I'm sure his own anger was justified. That is the extent of the blame I will take for what followed.

When the kid called me nigger lover, I didn't go angry, I went dark. Scary dark. A feeling I've only had a few times since. The simmering beneath the surface became hot. I could feel it in my skin. In my shaking hands. All the emotions from my freshman year came back. The helplessness. The aloneness. The lack of power. I didn't react at first. Didn't speak. I felt. I allowed the darkness to swallow me as the bell rang and students moved toward the bleachers for the assembly.

That moment would move me into a different future. This future. The future that has me writing this book with my black brother-in-law. My friend. My brother. That moment is when everything changed. It was the beginning. The true beginning of my *other* existence. I wonder now if that moment created my future or if my destiny created that moment.

That day I followed the kid to the drinking fountain. Another kid was in my ear egging me on. A devil on the shoulder. An instigator. Background noise. I can't see his face, but almost thirty years later I can still hear his obnoxious laugh. I can still see his Cheshire smile.

The punch echoed. I'd never felt more free. I don't ever again want to feel that free. The racist lay facedown on the gym floor, blood pooling around him, out cold. The gym was silent besides the hundreds of heads that snapped in the direction of the scene. At least that's how it felt. Like time had slowed down. I remember having a feeling that they were coming to get me. All of them. Pitch forks and hoes. A noose. My instinct was to run. I did. I made it to my locker before I was surrounded and grabbed, though I don't remember by who. Teachers? Students? Both? I'm not sure.

I was dragged to the office. A short time passed before an officer arrived and put me in handcuffs. They were cold and tight. They cut into my wrists. Crazy, I was being arrested, but all I could think about was basketball. At seventeen that's all I had. Without it what was I? I knew I'd be kicked off the team. The racist's mouth was ruined. I didn't care. Maybe when they sewed it back together he would reconsider how to use it. His lips opened into a half moon. Flesh exposed. His racism exposed. Newaygo's racism exposed. My anger exposed.

School officials showed me pictures, expecting to guilt me.

I laughed. *You made me this way,* I would have told them if I knew then what I know now. I didn't understand then the complexity of the experience my freshman year. I didn't understand the nature of the seed planted, the fear it produced, the bizarre dynamic that I've analyzed night after sleepless night throughout the years.

I don't trust white people. I don't trust me. I don't trust. I don't.

My last day at Newaygo High School was the last time I was ever called nigger lover to my face. The officer stared me down and told me I was being charged with assault and battery. What was the other kid charged with? He insulted and bashed. But I assaulted and battered. He threw the first punch with his mouth, but with his hands in his pockets. The fight ended in less than two seconds, but it had lasted more than two years.

As I write this I feel guilty. Guilty because I lost control. Guilty because we were both just kids, products of our experiences. The word may have been a word he'd grown up with. Exposed to by grandparents, parents, aunts, uncles, cousins, classmates, teachers, coaches. Maybe the word didn't come from his heart but from his roots.

But what happens when the roots find the heart? That boy is now a man and maybe he's used the "N" word again. Maybe multiple times. Maybe he's now a grandfather, father, uncle, cousin, teacher, or coach instilling broken values. Reinforcing the lessons he learned. I feel peace knowing he will never forget the consequences of using that word. Knowing he remembers my white fist. A white fist in defense of black oppression. I will swallow my guilt in the name of education.

My last day as a student at Newaygo High School, I stared at the officer attempting to intimidate me with threats of jail. *I've been in jail,* I should have told him. *Newaygo High School was my jail.* I think my demeanor said it. I think realizing my capacity for violence changed me. I think knowing I had the ability to hurt a person changed me. I know that day changed me. I knew then that I had changed. I won that moment. The officer looked away.

I was suspended ten days. There was a meeting scheduled to decide whether or not I would be expelled, but I never went to that meeting. I wasn't going back to that school. I told my parents that and they believed me. They knew. I think a parent always knows. My parents are good people. They were good people back then. But they were part of one America and I had dipped my toe in another. Back then they didn't understand.

I know it hurt my mom to sign over custody to Diane Cartwright. She did it for me, not because she thought that was what was best for me. That's love. I receive it as love. My mom knew how much basketball meant to me and because of the Michigan High School Athletic Association rules I would only be allowed to play for White Cloud High School if my legal guardian was a resident of White Cloud. That's how it happened. That's how a white boy ended up in a black home. For me, that was the beginning of my healing. The handcuffs on took the handcuffs off. I was free. I was a freed-man. I am free.

White Girls are Illegal

RAZEL JONES
WHITE CLOUD, MICHIGAN 1993

Summer of 1993. Just completed my senior year. Still in White Cloud, but mostly, looking forward to my departure. Those years from 7th grade to that last summer in White Cloud were about growth and development, through experiences. At that age, the experience that became the focal point for many boys, including me, was the experience of attraction, exploration, and interactions with girls. For the teenage me, and the other boys like me in my circle, all girls. Sometimes, any girl could become the object of our focus. For me. Black girls. Biracial girls. Filipino girls. Latina girls. White girls. Non-discriminatory. Welcoming all. Equal opportunity. For teenage me, beauty was beautiful in all its forms.

That summer, I was one step closer to my escape from the confines of parental guidance (PG). I was ready to see what un-restricted (R) life really was like. My PG was different than others' PG. My parents believed in force-fully guiding. They took that responsibility seriously. They guided me to church every Sunday. Not the, "Put in one hour and get it over with and get back to your day" type of church. We attended the, "You ain't gonna have no time to do nothin' else this weekend, so you might as well get comfort-able here" kind of church. Holiness church. Hand clappin', foot stompin', sanctified church.

Sunday after Sunday. Sunday School at 9:30 a.m. Sunday morning wor-ship service starting at 11 a.m. Take a break and have dinner, or was it lunch? Food in the fellowship hall in the back of the church when service was over, usually no earlier than 2 p.m. Then, the food. Fried chicken. Fried catfish. Spaghetti. Hot water cornbread. Macaroni and cheese. Collard greens. Mashed potatoes and gravy. Sweet potato pie, lemon cake, 7-Up cake. Hit the pop machine and place your two quarters in the recycled Vaseline bottle that had become the self-service cash register for the pop machine, a.k.a. old refrigerator. Red Pop. Rock & Rye. Not Sprite—we had Lemon-Lime.

Grape. Orange. Not Coke or Pepsi—we had Cola. If you know what I'm talking about, you were likely either poor, or black, or both.

This food. The aroma of the food first lured your attention away from your ability to focus on the interminable service. I was joined in that experience by Jevon, my friend turned brother. It was not uncommon for us to plot an intricate escape to the kitchen without being seen by our parents. We had to make our way to the built-on, annex, which included the fellowship hall and the kitchen.

Jevon was two years younger than me and through the years became my cellmate in the experience. We've had an inseparable bond and been in each other's lives for as long as I can remember. Through my younger years, all the way through high school, to Grand Valley, where we became roommates during my second year. Then, to Ferris State University in Big Rapids, where we transferred in 1997 to more deeply engage the beauty of the campus. That beauty, in the form of attractive black girls we encountered at special events we attended on the campus. They were our recruitment tours. Our admissions office. Camille, who would eventually become my wife, was one of those glorious beings. The recruitment tour that keeps on giving.

The smell of the food lured us out of the sanctuary. When we would successfully escape, usually through the guise of needing to use the men's bathroom—our best excuse—we would bee-line to the kitchen, hoping our parents would be so consumed with their praise they wouldn't notice our departure. We'd find a few mothers of the church preparing the feast, and beg them to have mercy on our poor, young, famished souls. Sometimes it would work. Mother Martin, or my godmother, Mother Jackson, would provide a small appetizer to hold us over until we could legally partake. Victuals.

Once we were finally, fully-authorized, through the lengthy blessing of the food, to indulge in the spread, we were too hungry to be connoisseurs. We ate so fast that we nearly forgot to chew what we'd consumed. We loaded more on our plates than we could handle. At the conclusion of the meal we were nearly in a coma. We would have to plot one more covert journey—the journey to the garbage with napkins strategically placed over our uneaten food to hide our waste. The adults were on the lookout for this signal, ready to chastise us for taking more than we could eat. "Don't you waste that food."

We didn't understand, at the time, that the provision of this food was a sacrifice of individuals' money, time, and energy. Many, without the resources to afford waste. Without the history of having an abundance to be able to waste. And, why in the world would we waste that heavenly, delectable buffet of love?

That meal. Prepared by the hands of skilled mothers of the church, well-versed in overtaking participants with post-dining paralysis. Slain in the spirit of gluttony. Our stillness compelled us to stay for a few more hours of evening service. If not our stillness, Brother and Sister Jones, and Jevon's parents, Brother and Sister Willis, mandated our return to the cell. That hard, wooden pew. Repentance was available from around 4-7 p.m.

At the end, we would stay, as our parents worked to handle the business of the church, while we took out trash, washed dishes, wiped down tables, and did whatever the adults in charge told us to do. The night would culminate with hours of sitting around in the fellowship hall, laughing, gossiping, cracking jokes, talking about current issues, talking about current people. "Child, did you see how fat so-and-so is getting? Might be a bun in that oven. Girl, you know they sleepin' together. They definitely ain't havin' no prayer service at each others' house at one in the morning."

Jevon, taking it all in to add to his daily comedy routine. Me, being admonished to stay out of grown folks' business. I was reminded, "Children are to be seen and not heard." That never jibed well for me. I longed to be heard. I long to be heard.

I'm sure there were other things to do, but there was no hurry to leave. On those days there was an opportunity to heal from the whiteness wounds, which had been inflicted Monday through Saturday. At that place, our blackness was celebrated.

The preacher was seen as the moral thought leader of the community. Our pastor, Pastor Robert E. Smith, Sr., was like a celebrity. Black people honored the man of God more than the President of the United States. Pre-Obama. The pastor was our leader. Throughout African American history, it was the black pastor that provided hope. Hope for slaves to be able to endure. Direction through the symbolic language of preaching to indicate to slaves plans for escape to the underground railroad. Post slavery, preachers kept providing hope. Hope for a better tomorrow. Our small black community within a community celebrated the uniqueness of relatable thought.

The melodic delivery of black preaching. "Somebody lift your hands and say yes!" The uplifting harmonies of the senior choir, accompanied by the blazing Leslie of the Hammond C-3; the rhythmic pulse of the shiny, blue Ludwig drum kit; the magical strings of the double-necked, custom, white guitar.

After the meal, it was not uncommon to find Jevon and I, lying asleep on the back wooden, un-cushioned pew. Sleeping through the storm of adulation, minor seventh chords, blues scale riffs, tuned-up, ear-grabbing preaching, and thunderous, responsive praise. How did I sleep through all of that? It was comfortable. I was comfortable.

So, we stayed until late into the night to prepare for the awaiting wounds that would appear when we came back to reality the next week. We'd come back throughout the week for additional treatment. Leaving meant we were one step closer to returning to vulnerability on our jobs, at our schools, in the grocery store. Vulnerability in White Cloud.

That summer after my high school graduation, I vowed that I would leave and not give my Sundays to that forced therapy. I would slip from under the thumbs of my PG parents and experience what I perceived as freedom. No rules. No curfews. No permission. No boundaries. No limits. No restrictions.

As has become normal in my life: man makes plans and God laughs.

The girl I was dating at the time, who I dated off and on from 7th grade through my first couple years of college, was Crystal Cartwright. She too, at times, attended the White Cloud Church of God in Christ. Crystal was one year behind me in school. Her mother, Diane became another mom to me. One of those women in the kitchen who would always sneak us the chicken leg and laugh as we scarfed it down. "Go somewhere with yo' lil' greedy selves." We'd laugh and follow the instructions. She was another mother to my generation. Crystal was the prettiest black girl I knew. Well, mostly black. Her mother was black.

Her father was a combination of races. There was some Native American, and a trace of black in there too. But, as far as I could tell, he was mostly white. You wouldn't have wanted to say that directly to him though. He would have resented that label. There's something about white men who seriously open up to black people. White people who become family to black people. There's another dimension of militance that emerges from them. They grip their anger with the system in ways black people are not allowed, in efforts to right the wrongs. Crystal's dad, Dennis, Sr. was the kind of white guy who would see those little statues of slave-like black men, holding lanterns in the yards of northern Michigan homes—lawn jockeys they were called. Dennis would become incensed. He became an abolitionist for black lawn jockeys everywhere he saw them, destroying them and leaving the evidence for the owners to pick up the pieces of their racist memorabilia.

Crystal's timing for getting serious about the church—about God—couldn't have been worse for my plans to experience freedom in college. I knew about God, but had determined that I wasn't ready to engage Him on a deeper level at that point in time. I'd stick to sometimes playing the drums, learning the organ, attending the services, and even though I was old enough not to take the back-row naps, I'd still find occasion to partake in the delight of the holy siesta.

Crystal was waking up. At one of those three-day revivals, she took the walk to the front of the church at the beckoning of the preacher and gave her life to God. I stayed put. I had plans. Damaged plans. We were supposed to party that summer.

By day three of the same revival. Sunday, July 25, 1993, my plans changed. I couldn't believe I was doing it. I was responding to the *call*. I was walking up the aisle. What about freedom? I would soon find out what real freedom was. I'm still enjoying that freedom. I'm still thankful for Crystal's decision, which influenced my decision.

This relationship with Crystal was not my only one. At that point, I was no longer chubby with squeezable cheeks. Basketball was no longer my favorite sport. I was a football player. A middle linebacker, #56 like Lawrence Taylor. I had slimmed down and toned up. One hundred sixty-five pounds of strength. Football ran through my bones. I had instincts for the game. I loved to hit and hit hard. Maybe it was a release of pent up aggression. Whatever it was, the released rage gave me peace and joy.

At 5 a.m. every weekday, Mr. Conklin—assistant principal, athletic director, and weight lifting enthusiast, would pick me up and we'd go to the weight room before school.

With the physical changes came a different sort of attention. Things had changed a lot since 3rd grade. Not everything changed though. That was long before cell phones, text messages, DMs. You couldn't even hit me on the hip on my pager yet. The main method of communication with most of the girls at the school was still those strategically folded, excessively creased letters—our SnapChat. I no longer tossed the letters at the subjects, I slipped them into hands as we passed in the hallway, allowing my hand to linger just long enough on theirs to indicate interest. Or if we sat in reach of one another in a classroom, I would write my observations in a personalized letter, as if painting a still-life portrait with adjectives. Capturing their beauty. Capturing their smile. Capturing their heart. When the authority figure at the front of the room would turn to the chalkboard, the handoff would happen, and their encapsulating short story would begin.

As I transitioned to those awkward teenage years, unlike others, I was losing my awkwardness. Developing physically yes, but just as important at the time, developing vocabulary. The contents of my letters no longer included checkboxes and drawings of hearts and stars. Words—I loved words.

In a letter, I was able to express what I was too timid to initially express face-to-face. I had time to think about the messaging and craft it in such a way that piqued interest. Curiosity. I wrote letters back and forth with lots of girls. Not just girls I dated. Not just girls I liked. Girls who were friends. While 3rd-grade Razel wanted everyone to think he believed girls to be yucky and boring, high-school Razel had changed the narrative. Beauty was beautiful.

I recall one time in early high school, a group of us black boys being told a story by a white coach and long-time teacher. This coach/teacher had been told that his daughter was receiving letters from a black guy. He looked at the group of young, black boys in the locker room, and made a statement teetering between micro and macro aggression. "It had to be from Raz; he's the only one of you that can write…"

I wasn't the only author. I remember my boy, Jemar (J.), a brother from Lansing who transplanted to White Cloud in 6th grade. His grandfather pastored the other black church in town—People's Baptist. He, and another brother who transplanted from Detroit, Antonio, and a few other brothers, including myself formed a group called Brothers in Christ (BIC), as if I wasn't already in church enough. It was a gospel group; we were all church boys, with varying levels of commitment to God, but corresponding levels of being forced to be in church. We toggled between believing we were the rural doppelgangers for R&B's Boyz II Men and contemporary gospel's Commissioned. It depended on if the audience was people from the local churches or girls from the local schools.

Antonio and I intercepted a letter J. had written to one of the girls at school. The words of J.'s letter were pure copyright infringement as he had inserted the words to one of Commissioned's gospel songs to the Lord, but directed the lyrics at the girl's heart. "Rain fills the sky, yet the sun is always there though it seems to hide—waiting for the right moment to brighten up your life…I will be that and much more, if you only give me half a chance." Letters were our vehicle to the hearts of young ladies.

Third-grade Jessica eventually rejected her mother's previous instruction and found herself checking *yes* to one of J.'s requests. In 9th grade, they dated. At that point, I was well beyond the 3rd-grade feelings. We were all friends. We were freshmen then. I remember walking down Lester Street after school one day. Jessica, J., me, and a half-Filipino, half-white cheerleader friend of mine. We walked down that street listening to music on a Walkman with a built-in speaker, gathering close to one another and singing our hearts out. The lyrics to Bobby Brown's, *Roni*. "My heart belongs to tenderoni, she's my only love…She's a special kind of girl that makes her daddy feel proud; you know the kind of girl that stands out in crowds…"

A few years later, in the summer before my junior year, J. and I walked that familiar path from the school to the Lester Street apartments that J. called home. That time, we were accompanied by another of our boys, Tony Gates. He lived between Las Vegas and White Cloud over the years and was part of a large family of black people who called White Cloud home. Along with the three of us young, black guys were two white girls. I can't remember who they were. I can't remember what they were doing, but I soon found out that…

White girls are illegal.

As we strolled down Lester Street, having a good time, the sounds of our laughter and joy were interrupted as the space was infiltrated by the timbre of police sirens and the swirl of lights.

The local officer we knew all too well. He was called anytime someone white felt fear or annoyance about someone black. He was on-the-scene when a disgruntled white dad from the community came to the Mill Pond, where all the black kids hung out, and began firing his weapon, frustrated because his daughter had decided to reenact a real-life version of Spike Lee's, *Jungle Fever*. That cop was never there for us. He was always there because of us.

He would often pull me over as I drove my mom's 1990 Chevy Corsica. No infraction. No legitimate suspicion. Just pulled me over. He knew the car. He knew me. I knew him. He seemed to always know where I was. Who could I tell? Who would do anything about it? He didn't like me and the feeling was mutual. He didn't like my kind and my kind didn't like him. In the first few encounters, I followed the preparation my dad had given me. I talked with respect. Yes, sir. How may I help you, sir? No, sir, I don't know why you stopped me.

Be still. Be alert. Be aware. Be cool.

I was trained. In those early days, I was practicing. But, the encounters became unbelievably frequent. The respect for that cop waned. He harassed us that day. There was no need for the chirp of his siren or for the flash of his lights. He told us some bogus statute. "You are not allowed to have more than three people walking in a group in town."

"What? Are you kidding me? In this town?" He had never mentioned that statute as I rode bikes with gangs of white kids since those early elementary days. Never. We had more than three people in a group walking every day. Everyone had more than three people walking in a group every day. "Leave us alone. Go find something to do."

His real problem was not the number of us, but the composition of us. Three black boys, two white girls. See, what you have to understand…

White girls are illegal.

J. and I rejected his warning and began to continue on our path. Tony though, had a few more words for the cop. Tony scolded him and informed him that his father was an attorney in Las Vegas and that he knew his rights. The cop retreated. But, we all knew we would see him again. We always did. Especially if we were in the company of white girls.

Another reminder.

A friend of mine from kindergarten—a guy—had been dating another friend from kindergarten—a girl. Both had roots in the area. Their parents grew up around the time my parents grew up in the area. I had spent years in friendship with her. I knew her parents and siblings. Her parents expressed that they thought of me as highly respectful and respectable. Artic-

ulate. That verbal ability within some black people that always seems to surprise some white people. Microaggression.

Anyway, they thought I was intelligent. They thought I was a good guy.
They knew my family to be a positive presence in the community. My dad
served on various boards in the community, including the White Cloud
School Board from 1983 until around 2013. Mom served on the White
Cloud Community Library Board for around seven years. Caring for the
community. Giving time to make the place better. Advocating for the rights
of the underserved.

Then, juniors in high school. That teenage girl, who had been my class-
mate since kindergarten was a part of the group of girls who had begun to
acknowledge the physical changes that had occurred in me over the past few
years. She expressed that appreciation with flirting and words of affirma-
tion. I was inclined to accept the words, not fully thinking of the impact my
acceptance would have on my male friend.

He heard of the exchange. Red with anger. *How could she choose black over
me*, must have been his thought. Damaged, he ended their relationship. Then
his attention turned to me. Ready to fully engage me, I saw him coming and
thought for him, *you don't want to do this.* A discussion would begin. I was all
for discussions. But, in that discussion, his vocabulary was limited. He
wanted to stir me to violence. He wanted to make me feel. He wanted me to
know my place. But, he only had one word.

"Nigger!"

Nigger...It felt sharper than normal. It wasn't friendly from a friend. The
laughable part is that's all he had. The moniker passed down from his great,
great, grandfather and them. It had made its way to another generation of
limited thinkers. Limited speakers. Limited young men. Limited. That's all he
had. He didn't have the words. He didn't have the power. He didn't have
control.

I'm not denying some fault in the situation. I should have rejected her
advances, instead of entertaining them—sixteen-year-old me did not reject
the newfound attention. Maybe it was because I had been rejected for so
long. I was in a time and position where I was more inclined to reject rejec-
tion and accept acceptance. I was caught off-guard by his outburst. I
could've fought him, but I was more hurt than angry. Since kindergarten we
had been friends. Yet, the length of friendship did not change the fact that...

White girls are illegal.

Hurt people, hurt people. That day I felt motivated to carry that relationship further. Vindictive. Until her parents demanded we didn't. I was annoyed by their response to me. I was considered great to them up until the crossover. Respectful. Respectable. Athletic. Intelligent. Articulate...I should have seen it coming.

The descriptors changed. Not good enough for our daughter. Out-of-line. Unwelcomed. Off-limits. Black. In their eyes, I quickly went from being a good kid, to being a black kid. Were those opposites? I was allowed at their home until their home developed interest in me. What changed? It wasn't me. I didn't change. I believe what changed was their perspective that my blackness felt somehow transferable. From their lens, I would ruin her life. I would bring danger to their family, even though I wasn't dangerous. I wasn't a threat. It's just...

White girls are illegal.

Could it be that it was not me they were really worried about? Could it be that they were more concerned about other people's reactions to me? They feared having to introduce me at the family gatherings. Having to teach their network how to pronounce my ethnic name. Fear that the relationship might work and they'd have a Razel, Jr. as their grandson one day. Fear of having to come out of their comfort zones and dip a toe into my world. Maybe? I don't know. But, I do know, they feared. They persuaded. They attempted. They acted. It didn't work.

It just didn't work. For me. I remember going to the movies with her in Fremont, the city where I was born. The city Daniel was born. Just fourteen miles from home. Not home. My first Dutch environment. Whiter than White Cloud. As we were selecting movies, I was surprised and excited to see my favorite actor's latest movie at the theater. That theater barely ever carried black films. But, somehow—for some reason—that time, of all the movies, they were showing Denzel Washington in *Malcolm X*. "Give me two tickets and a box of popcorn, please!" I had been waiting to see that movie.

We entered the theater. Walking to our seats, I quickly became fully aware of all eyes on me. That was nothing new, as you develop a shoulder-shrugging comfort with all eyes being on you when you are one of a limited number of black people in a white community. In Fremont, of all places. That day was different though. The theater was nowhere near full. I imagine there weren't that many people in Fremont who wanted to see Malcolm X. There were, however, more black people in the theater than white. The difference in the eyes that gripped me as I entered the theater was that they were not the eyes of white people. Those were eyes that looked more like my eyes. The eyes of the few black patrons who had found their seats before me asked the question, "What is he doing bringing a white girl to watch Malcolm X?" Tension. Tension that would become worse after the movie. The movie was long and uncomfortable. Three hours— about the length of one of those church services. Painful. Painfully long, given my company. Painfully good. Amazingly real. Real eye opening. The problem...

Her eyes weren't opened. After the movie, instead of discussing, I was explaining. It wasn't her fault. It was her reality. I started to believe that she wasn't going to be a partner in rebelling against the system of oppression me and Malcom faced. Instead, for her, it seemed to be more about rebelling against just her parents. That was the beginning of the end of the adventure for me.

White girls are illegal.

Illegal until recently. Miscegenation. The mixing of types of people. Races of people. The cohabitation or intermarriage between racial groups was not fully legal in all U.S. states until 1967; 1967 was not long ago. My dad graduated from high school in 1962. He was a grown man with a career, wife, and four children by 1967, but white girls were literally illegal. It was illegal in twenty-two states, at the time of his graduation from high school, to marry someone of another race. It took a Supreme Court ruling to declare those laws unconstitutional in 1967 and change the course of history.

I'm so glad it changed. Without the change, my nephews and nieces would be illegal. Crystal would be illegal. Daniel's marriage to my sister-in-law, Vanessa would be illegal. Daniel's beautiful children would be illegal. My brother, Jerome and Janna's children would be illegal. Jevon's marriage to Dena would be illegal. Their beautiful children would be illegal. So much of God's beauty would be illegal.

In fact, I would have a criminal record. For every time I explored beauty outside of my race. This chapter would have given me more than three strikes. I would have failed my background check for breaking a law that should never have been a law in the first place. A law, like the one the cop made up to harass us with on Lester Street.

There are times when it is critical for the government to intervene. To take action to right the wrongs of human error. Human bias. Human fear. Human hate. To look at the common views of citizens and say, I know what you want. I know what ideals you are protecting. I know you do not want to change. But, this is not right. This has to change.

Change is coming. We demand it. We demand Change.

As we sit on the edge of reform of policing in America, we are once again at a spot in our history where government needs to intervene. Too often, black and brown people are unjustly killed, harassed, and discriminated against at the hands of biased, overpowered citizens who have been deputized as police.

Too many times, people of color are the victims of choke holds, knees to the neck, and kill shots—situations that could've been handled differently. Brutality that never had to happen. There were other options. There were better practices. Continuing to allow it to be okay for disproportionate numbers of brutal, unnecessary interactions is unacceptable. We won't accept it. We will vote. We will protest. We will declare. We will stand. Against injustice. Against inequity. Against bias. Against hate. Against the abuse of power. Against racism. Sentencing without trials. Murders, because of bad policies. Lack of training. Unchecked biases. It's not just that we want better. We demand better. Anything less is unacceptable. Anything less is too little.

Anything less is ridiculous.

As ridiculous as the title of this chapter.

White girls are illegal.

Black Love

DANIEL ABBOTT
WHITE CLOUD, MICHIGAN 1994

In the weeks following my arrest I'd been to court twice. The assault and battery charges stuck. I was given the choice of three days in jail or twenty hours of community service. I chose the latter and months later, when the weather swayed warm, I would serve my time painting curbs yellow in downtown White Cloud.

My second time in court my parents signed over custody to Diane Cartwright. Diane was all business at the proceedings. Showing the world what she always showed the world: Nothing. She was a black woman taking on the legal responsibility of raising a white child, yet she showed no visible emotion. Stone-faced, but with this defiant strength, like it was the world that had failed, not me. Like she would fix the mess that Newaygo made of me.

My mom was teary-eyed and reluctant, but had strength of her own. She let me go because she wanted me to graduate high school. School of choice was more difficult to get back then. I'd learn later that she'd sometimes cry on the drive home after coming to visit me in White Cloud. I was her oldest child. I was her son, she told me, and she wanted me home. She didn't understand that for the first time since we left Grand Rapids, I was home. That battered trailer in White Cloud was home.

We lived poor on Tulip Street. Back then food stamps were still paper. We peeled them from our pockets and swallowed the judgmental looks from white cashiers in White Cloud grocery stores. Eyes trying to figure me out. Mom Cartwright with that thousand-mile stare. A look that said she'd been around the block and back. And back around the block again. Those that thought they were better than us were beneath her. That's what her eyes told me. Those dying to ask questions about the white son with the black mother, me bagging her groceries, carrying her groceries, calling her Ma. Those questions weren't asked. Not to Diane Cartwright. Her demeanor let the world know there would be no questions. No answers. Give me my change and get to steppin'. Just give me my change.

That was for people who didn't matter. If Diane Cartwright loved you, she spoke her mind whether you were interested in hearing it or not. Her delivery had an edge, like her voice had a scowl. When she was mad at you she'd get quiet for a while and comments would leak out a little at a time, beneath her breath, almost like she was arguing with two halves of her whole self. Then, once that argument was settled, she came at you full-force, mostly making no sense. Diane Cartwright wasn't the most articulate person when she was pissed off and she wasn't one to apologize with words, only with actions. She'd cook for you, give you a few dollars, but she never said I'm sorry. I knew Diane Cartwright for almost thirty years and I cannot recall a time she said the words, *I'm sorry*. Not to me; not to anyone else.

Diane was a single mother of four. Crystal, my age, was a grade ahead of me in school. Latrice was two years younger than me. Denny was twelve then and Kandi was nine when I moved into the Cartwright home in 1994.

After moving in, it didn't take long for Denny and I to become brothers. We slept foot to head in his twin-sized bed. We sang 90s R&B songs off-key, taking turns on the solo parts, doing the chorus together. Song after song: "Gangsta Lean" by DRS, "If I Ever Fall in Love Again" by Shai, "Bump N' Grind" by R. Kelly. We'd go on like that until we heard Mom's footsteps, until she'd yell from the back room for us to "Shut the hell up!" Or, "Denny, shut your black ass up." Always followed by a long pause. She was probably lighting a Newport. Probably shaking her head the way she liked to do before she smiled. Half-joking, half-serious. Denny and I would fill that space with laughter. "Dee, you can shut your white ass up too!"

It was wintertime when I moved into that trailer on Tulip Street. We made a basketball hoop out of a bent metal coat hanger and wedged it in the front door. We played one-on-one with a wad of socks folded into a ball, pretending to dribble, shooting jumpers from across the room. I was still able to bully Denny a little back then. Dunk after dunk until he got mad. Until he stepped onto the black marble coffee table and drop-kicked me in the jewels. Denny laughed at me when I collapsed onto the floor. He's still laughing at me today. We still laugh about that incident today.

Latrice and I were friends before I moved in. She was dating Robert Trice, a friend of mine, and one of Stevie's teammates at that basketball tournament where we met in Kent City a few years before. Latrice and I moved in the same circles. We grew closer in my time at the house. Got in trouble together for missing curfew. Got put on punishment together. Faced Mom's wrath together. Years later our kids would grow up together. They'd grow up as cousins. Get into trouble of their own.

Kandi was my baby sister. In those years at the Cartwrights', on those nights when Stevie couldn't leave the house or I didn't feel like going out, I spent time with Kandi. We'd play two-hand Spades, Rummy, or Monopoly, though we were hardly ever able to get through a game without arguing. Sometimes I'd let her climb on my back when I did push-ups. We'd eat snacks. Watch movies. We'd hang. Me and baby sister would hang.

Crystal wasn't home much. She was a senior at White Cloud and focused on her grades and church and Razel. Raz was dating Crystal at the time. He was in his freshman year at Grand Valley State University. My earliest memories of Raz are of him pulling up in a white Ford Ranger to pick up Crystal for whatever mischief they were into then. He'd bring Kandi string cheese. He'd wrestle with Denny. Show him that Jones strength, when Denny tried him. Denny always liked to try him.

I'd see Razel on Sundays too. He played keys at The Church of God in Christ, the rickety God shack Mom Cartwright dragged us to every Sunday. Whoever was home on Sunday morning had to go. Somehow it was always me. Or Stevie if he stayed the night on Saturday, which he often did. The Cartwright kids usually found a way to be gone, but I didn't know any better. Church was murder. Hard wooden pews. Hours and hours of preaching. Elder Smith had a way of piercing your soul with his eyes. Made you feel like you did something wrong and had you analyzing your week. The scent of food cooking in the kitchen. The pangs of the stomach. The wait to eat was excruciating.

I coped by bringing a notebook. I wrote raps in the back of the sanctuary. Basketball raps. Anger raps. Fighting raps. A couple years later Razel and I would record a gospel song together. He'd lay the track and I'd spit over the beat. Our boy Jemar (J.) would sing the vocals. Connections, man. So many connections. God works in intentional ways.

For years Razel and I would be out of touch. Eventually we'd marry sisters. I'd become the white uncle to his beautiful black daughter, Kayden. He'd become the black uncle to my eight beautiful biracial children. My four biracial suns. My four biracial moons. Back then though, what I remember most about Raz is that he was always there for Mom Cartwright. Always there for the family. Always. He was there. He'd take Mom to the doctor, or to get groceries. He'd bring Latrice home from basketball practice, volleyball practice, track practice. Raz was always around. A provider even at that young age. A manchild. I looked up to him. Still look up to him.

Raz was different. He was definitely different. Razel Jones is definitely different.

I remember one night I came home and Mom was asleep on the couch with a cigarette hanging from her mouth. An arc of ash hung from a Newport butt. Her mouth was half open. Her eyes rolled back in her head. Because her chest rose and fell I knew she was alive. I plucked the cigarette butt from her lips and dropped it into the ashtray atop a graveyard of other nubbed-out corpses. I blew the ashes off her t-shirt and covered her with a blanket. I sat at her feet and watched her sleep. I didn't yet know about the debilitating headaches. About the other things. The vices. All I knew was I loved her and I didn't want to see her in pain.

We lived poor.

I remember one time Mom Cartwright needed a ride to the hospital and didn't have a car. She seemed to never have a car. That day she didn't have the gas money her so-called friend required for the fifteen-mile drive to Fremont. This so-called friend lived down the street from us. It was wintertime. Their driveway had already been plowed. I helped Mom Cartwright shovel their yard because work was required from this so-called friend. This woman watched from the window while Mom and I shoveled snow off her grass. Mom listened to me complain about the absurdity of what we were doing, but she didn't join in.

Mom Cartwright did what the white woman required.

We never had much, but we never went hungry. Mom always came up with the $3 admission to my basketball games my senior year at White Cloud. She never missed a game. Never held her tongue. Ignored the plays that brought the crowd to their feet and focused instead on the times I forgot to box out, or the times I'd stop to talk trash instead of getting back on defense. Mom Cartwright told it as she saw it. Never sugar coated. Never watered down.

I'd go on to make all-area honorable mention. We'd beat Newaygo for the conference championship and I'd drop sixteen points, eight rebounds, and eight assists. I'd shake hands with my former teammates, guys who played no role in my negative experience at that school. The coach would look away when I approached him in that sportsmanship line. He wouldn't shake my hand. I made sure to find his eyes during our celebration, when it was my turn to cut down the net. He didn't return my smile. Well, my smirk, if I'm being honest.

I lived with the Cartwrights for over two years. I revisit those years often. I think about that transitional period in my life. The Newaygo experience, the seed of distrust for people with white skin. The safety I felt in Diane Cartwright's home. The love.

I'd go on to date the full spectrum of women: black, biracial, Puerto Rican, Costa Rican, Mexican, Korean, the occasional white girl. But I married a black woman. My wife is a black woman. I feel safe with a black woman. I feel understood with a black woman. I know that comfort was developed during my time in the Cartwright house. I came into Diane Cartwright's home low, confused, and uncomfortable in my skin. She showed me love during a time when I felt unloved. Stitches on wounds. A soul hug. I was allowed to breathe. I breathed.

As I write this Diane Cartwright has been gone just over five months. This is hard to write. Not because Mom has moved on; everyone moves on. Not because I miss her; of course I miss her. But because I'd allowed the busyness of my life to get in the way of picking up a phone. Because I never took the time to take the short drive up US-131 to visit her in Cedar Springs where she'd lived the last several years of her life around her daughters, her sons-in-law, and her grandkids.

I never thought to ask her why she took me in. Why she took a chance on the white boy with the hot temper. Why when she barely had enough for her own children, she found enough for me. I never told her what she meant to me. I never knew what I meant to her. I don't know if I was different than the countless other knuckleheads she mothered over the years. I do know that I was the only one legally hers. I know she believed I was worth it. That I was better than the way I was perceived by the world. The way I perceived myself. She saw the best in me before I saw the best in me.

I was broken when I met her and to say she fixed me would be an exaggeration. I'm still fixing me. My wife is fixing me. My children are fixing me. God stays fixing me. I'm still not fixed. I am and always will be a work-in-progress. What's not an exaggeration is that a black woman showed a white boy unconditional love. A black woman taught a white boy how to unconditionally love. Diane Cartwright saw me as God sees me: as a masterpiece.

The last time I saw Diane Cartwright alive was at Razel's brother's funeral in July of 2019. It was a hard day. Razel is a strong man. He's always been a strong man. Seeing him hurt the way he hurt that day was difficult. Mom sat beside me and my wife Vanessa and our son Jude. She didn't hold my distance against me. We settled in beside each other because we'd always settled in beside each other. After the service I hugged her and kissed her on the cheek. She scolded me about not bringing her grandbabies around. I smiled. Started to make an excuse before she cut me that eye. The same eye she used to cut me when I was seventeen and learning her pet peeves: I better speak when I come in the house. Don't set my hat on her table. Say "huh" don't say "what."

The last words I said to Diane Cartwright were I love you.

She said she loved me back.

What an honor that she loved me back.

I'm Not Different

RAZEL JONES
WHITE CLOUD, MICHIGAN 2013

Throughout my time growing up in White Cloud, there were countless conversations where a white child…later a white preteen…later a white teenager…later a white young adult…even later, at a twenty-year class reunion, a white grown man, without so much growth, would let that ultra-offensive term roll off of the tongue. In my presence. Nigger this or nigger that, followed by a "No-offense, Raz," or an "I don't mean you, Razel."

When I was old enough to better understand the significance, I developed a variety of responses. Yelling, fighting, cussing, crying, dismissing. Dismissing. It happened so often that a large part of me became immune. I thought. Conditioned from the beginning of my development to hear *nigger*, without offense. Eventually offended through the exception statement as much as the slur.

When I recall the frequency, the comfort held by speakers who allowed the viscous slight to part their lips, the degradation that these simple minds somehow thought could be aimed to circumvent me, like a heat-seeking missile, while landing on other intended black people, I lament. I lament that I didn't have the skillset I now have to educate them. I lament that I allowed the conditioning to keep me from consistently feeling the offence that should have taken me over, moving me into a self-righteous anger. I lament. I lament that no authority figure, who at some point had to have heard the term, as it acutely draws the attention of the ear-gate with its sharpness, did anything about it. Its piercing impact. Its hateful movement. Someone had to hear. I lament. I lament that I was often so avoidant of punishment that I didn't address those oversteps, and accept whatever level of detention, suspension, or expulsion would have come as a prize for the act. I lament.

I lament that I, at times, in a way that now sickens me, found comfort in the explanation that the term wasn't meant to be applied to me. My childish mind wanted to believe that maybe I am different. After all, life had already begun to show me that I'm definitely different…

I'm not different.

I am no exception.

Just because you know me does not mean that I am not black. I am black. I am thankfully black. I am black just like the person you are hurling your insult at. On the way to them, it hits me. I'm Colin Kaepernick black. Protesting oppression black. Not-so-sure about the *National Anthem* black. Skeptical of the *Pledge of Allegiance* black. I'm George Floyd black. At times, leery of law enforcement black. Don't trust the system black.

I'm not different.

I am no exception.

I have the same skin. The same color. The same history. The same disdain. The same.

I'm not different.

I am no exception.

I lament that even at a twenty-year class reunion when pulled into a conversation by this grown-ish man. His name is inconsequential, but his impact was not. I let the use of *nigger* slide again. By that time, I was a professional communicator. I was a diversity advocate. I did the work. I had the knowledge. I could have addressed it intellectually. I should have addressed it somehow.

Earlier in my adult life I chased down a passerby in a pickup truck on Lake Michigan Drive on my way to a class at Grand Valley State University. This man brandished his representative Confederate flag in the back of his pickup truck as he passed by. He, for no reason at all, felt the urge to roll his window down to yell that taunting term…"Nigger!" For no reason at all. For some reason. For a definite reason. That day, I snapped. I chased him down. Onto a backroad. Without restraint. Without fear of consequence. Without backup. Off the route that was leading me to my class. My education could wait; his needed to begin.

The coward sped off, winding down back roads in a Dukes of Hazzard type chase scene. I was in hot pursuit. I was hot. Boiling. Burning. There is a rage that can overtake you that makes consequences irrelevant. I didn't care if he had a weapon. He probably did. I imagined it a prerequisite for Confederate membership to carry a big gun in your big truck. I didn't care.

The coward escaped.

I have long understood that you can't fight every battle. Every fight doesn't change a situation. Sometimes, the wise decision is to walk away. Doing so, however, is not always easy. With maturity, that rage is quieted, but not erased. As I have matured, I have learned that some fights aren't worth my time. My energy. My truth. Some conversations aren't worthy of my contribution. I can tell you the truth, but if you aren't primed to receive the truth, the truth won't matter. To you. For you. It won't matter. If it doesn't matter, why do I care to invest my energy. My time. My truth. I get to control what I invest in. Who I invest in. I determine if it is worth my investment. I have learned that I may be able to knock the racist down, but when he gets up, he will just be a beat up, refueled racist. I have not chased down any more trucks. I have learned to consider consequences. I have learned that my strength is not in my ability to win a fight, but in my ability to influence a mind.

As I approached my twenty-year class reunion, I was excited to reconnect with my childhood friends. I hadn't made it to any of the other reunions to that point. I was one of those people who wanted to have some things in place before reuniting. By the time of the ten-year reunion, I was twenty-seven, and didn't have much of anything together in my life. No house. No degree. No fine job. No children. No wife. The things you feel matter when you think you understand more about life than you actually do. By the time of the twenty-year reunion more of that stuff was in place. I had a house. A Bachelor's degree. Was working on my MBA. Had a good HR job. Had my almost one-year-old daughter, Kayden. And, I had a wife. I had the wife. An incredible wife.

Camille.

Camille would absolutely rock a reunion, but she chose not to go. Camille is an amazing, classy African American woman. Flowing hair. Caramel skin. Deep brown eyes. My wife has the kind of beauty that stands out in a crowd. Tenderoni. She's impressive. Camille walks into a room with that Michelle Obamaesque poise. Never appearing intimidated. Never out of her element. An intriguing conversationalist to boot. She rode with me to White Cloud but opted to stay at my parents' house with our new baby instead of attending the reunion. She didn't like bringing our daughter in crowds or leaving her with other people. Plus, this would give her an opportunity to relax; something that is tough to come by as a new mom.

By the time of the reunion, I had thoughtfully addressed others who used the word. I had fought over the word. I had taken action over the word. But, something about that reunion experience drew me back to the paralyzed, non-responsive state I had been conditioned to evoke throughout that complicated childhood. Temporary insanity. The term typically used to describe someone in a snapped state of being. The true insanity for me was not snapping. Letting things go that I could have addressed. Temporary apathy. Followed by permanent regret.

While it is true that you must choose your battles, there are some battles that need to be fought to protect your own dignity. To protect the next person who will experience the same pattern from the same source, if unchecked. There are some people who can learn the lesson from you, productively. There are some people who are not lost causes. They just need direction. Instruction. Insight. Understanding. They just don't get it, but they could.

At the class reunion, that was a battle worth choosing, yet I had made a decision to let it go. It felt easier. It would have taken so much energy. So much effort. So much explanation. So much time. I was at a class reunion. I preferred to use that limited time, like the kids at recess preferred to get right to their activities of adventure, exploration, and escape. That day, I didn't care to fix him, even though I may have been positioned to do so. I could feel a strange, yet honest openness to me.

I wasn't there for that. Not that day. I was there for a reunion. I was uniting again with the parts of my experience, the people of my experience I wished to connect with. I didn't wish to be in union again with those feelings. I chose escape. There were no more conversations with that guy. With that past. Not on that day.

If Camille was there, I probably would have addressed it differently. Probably worse. I couldn't have allowed her to watch me stand there and accept the use of the term in her presence. I would have had to address it. Otherwise, *she* would have addressed it. She would have found the energy to teach him. That's probably why she chose not to go. She didn't feel like it that day. There are days when you just don't feel like it. When I arrived back at my parents' house, and Camille asked how the reunion went, my answer was simple. Undetailed. Unwilling to force her to relive her negative experiences through mine. The typical answer of a man who had just battled oppression, stress, annoyance, and the like and is asked by his wife how the day went.

Fine. It was fine. It wasn't fine. It was both. It was my normal, abnormal White Cloud experience.

At that reunion, my classmates and I relived our White Cloud experience—discussed our White Cloud education. That education consisted of many subjects. Algebra, Literature, Government, U.S. History, Geography, PE, Geometry, Drama. Probably most importantly though, Cross Cultural Navigation. I could flow between different people groups seemingly seamlessly. It looked natural to some as they watched me. As they watch me. But, it wasn't natural. It isn't natural. It was learned. It was my White Cloud education. It wasn't normal.

Abnormal.

College. Adulthood. Professional career. Ministry. Authoring. The White Cloud experience. That education. That abnormal extended social experiment, called my upbringing, has stayed with me. The ability I have gained to flow between audiences, without fear of the racial construction of the group has caused the *abnormal* to become *normal* for me.

I can maneuver between the lines of culture. I code-switch without knowing I have. Sometimes frustrated that I did it again. I have the ability, but over the years I have lost the desire. For so many years, I lived as two Razels. One: The Razel who at first glance made white people uncomfortable. Two: The Razel who at first glance made black people uncomfortable. One: The Razel who liked to listen to AC/DC's *Thunderstruck*. Two: The Razel who grooved while listening to LL Cool J's *Mama Said Knock You Out*. One: The Razel who could command the vocabulary of Standard American English with ease, to the point that he went to University and earned a degree in the language. Two: The Razel who could switch into comfortably playing the dozens with a group of black friends and family, thoughtlessly using the appropriate Ebonic dialect of the day.

It was in White Cloud where I started to learn how to make both white and black people comfortable. College gave me a lab to refine the skills. My professional career, a field to try my proven experimental data in real life.

I made you comfortable. That's why you're still reading. I'm accessible to you. That's why you're still here.

So, now that I have your attention. Let me say this one more time…maybe two.

I'm not different.

I'm no exception.

I want you to examine your comfort with me. You're comfortable with me because you have either gotten to know me in real life, or you have started to know me through the pages of this book. You aren't threatened by me. You understand that I'm a human being, like you are. You understand that I love my family, like you love your family. You understand that I have feelings and emotions, like you have feelings and emotions. You understand that I have a history, like you have a history. You understand that I want a future, like you want a future. You understand that I'm not perfect.

Neither are you.

I apologize up-front for the generalization, but in general…something I've found about many white people in my life is that they *accept* me, then they *except* me. This is a practice I call *Cultural Exceptionism*.

Because they are comfortable with me, they believe what I say about race, while assuming that others are making things up. Because they know me, they are prone to listen to me more. Because I know how to make them comfortable, I am more likely to be heard. They. Some. Accept me.

Maybe your experience hasn't been with me. Perhaps you are the white grandparent of a cross-culturally adopted child. I have seen this powerful relationship melt cold, formerly unreceptive hearts. True love opens individuals up to see the error of their thoughts. Their ways. Their biases. Don't stop there. Don't stop at the person you open up to. Keep going.

It has always been my hope that once accepted, I would have the ability to infiltrate those closed-off spaces in the heads of the white people I'm connected to and pry their minds open, ushering in an acceptance of more than just me. Unfortunately, many individuals' minds don't open past me. Many people's minds don't open beyond the one or two *others* they have relationship with.

Instead of a transformation of your default view of *other* because of your safe, productive experience with me, after accepting me, next you except me. You make me an exception, instead of changing your default. *Cultural Exceptionism.*

If you have had a positive experience with me in life; if you have had a good experience with me in this book, there is just one thing I ask of you in response. One thing. Stop excepting and start accepting. Change your default. Take the risk of expecting the next black man you encounter to more likely be an opportunity than a threat. Productive rather than pitiful. Human rather than hurtful. Dependable rather than destructive. A man, rather than a menace. Change your default. It's true, some will let you down. Some of your race have let you down too. But, your default view of your race hasn't likely changed.

There is no doubt in my mind that you have had some positive experiences with a phenomenal person of color. It is likely that you have encountered the amazingness, the charisma, the intelligence, the contribution, the talent, the beauty of a person of color. I'm willing to bet that you have come across someone who has shattered your pre-existing stereotypes and demonstrated a conflicting and positive reality of the remarkable character of some person of color.

I'm not different.

I'm no exception.

It Never Rains in Southern California

DANIEL ABBOTT
SAN DIEGO, CALIFORNIA 1996

We fasted the first forty-eight hours of Marine Corps boot camp. The immunizations required it, though that torture was never fully explained. I had a reaction to the shots and hours after the plane touched down in San Diego I was praying to porcelain, vomiting my last Michigan meal.

I'd shaved my head bald with a disposable razor in the airport bathroom. The United States Marine Corps didn't care. During processing the barber let the hot steel teeth of the clippers drag across my scalp and break the skin. Even after drawing blood, the barber wiped the clippers with his apron and continued. Every man would be given the same treatment. Each recruit would have to endure every boot camp thing there was to endure.

We sat in what the Marines called A to B, criss-cross applesauce, in formation, knees touching the ribs of the recruit in front of us. For hours we sat like that and waited. I was barely conscious and too weak to hold my head up, so it rested on the camouflaged back of the recruit in front of me.

We marched to station after station during processing. I staggered, struggling to stay on my feet. The California heat didn't help. I was dehydrated and weak. I grabbed and I leaned, but I didn't fall. And when those forty-eight hours were over, when the sickness subsided, when my strength was returning, we marched to our first meal of Marine Corps boot camp.

The first time Snipes pushed me, I let it slide. He'd marched behind me the previous two days watching me struggle, annoyed I was slowing him down. He was a Texas kid with a small-town vibe. Newaygo South. There perhaps, because his daddy, granddaddy, and great granddaddy had all been Marines. One of those Hoorah, Devil Dog! types. Semper Fi. Uniform perfect. Boots with a flawless spitshine.

The second time Snipes pushed me, I felt that Newaygo anger begin to surface. An anger I hadn't yet tamed at nineteen. A temper that would get a gun drawn on me at age twenty-three, a dumb temper, the kind of temper that would see the gun and keep coming forward until a friend grabbed me from behind and dragged me away.

Hunger and heat. That Newaygo anger. I turned over my shoulder and gave Snipes a not-so-subtle look that said don't.

The third time Snipes pushed me the platoon had halted. I didn't hear the command and slammed into the recruit in front of me. Snipes bumped me with his forearm. Then he shoved me and called me some sort of derogatory small-town Texas slang. I can't recall his words. That third time though, I turned over my shoulder and said, "Touch me again and I'll put you to sleep." I let him consider my words. Allowed him to swell with Marine Corps killer pride. Honor. Courage. Commitment. Uptight. Obedient.

As a young child my great-grandmother told me the only way to deal with a bully was to punch him in the nose. When I was a teenager, 2Pac told me to bomb first. The incident in Newaygo, that punch that echoed throughout the gym, taught me another lesson. That sometimes violence solves problems. Word travels through small towns. After that incident in Newaygo, no one ever tried me in Newaygo County again. Not with words; not with actions.

Recruit Snipes pushed me one final time that day in Southern California.

When my fist crashed against his temple his body went limp and he fell onto the grass. Gone. I was gone too. In darkness. In that scary place that violence takes me. I considered myself then, and I consider myself now, a moral man. But in that moment, I had no moral constraints. I approached Snipes with the intention, I think now, of ending his life. The world was pinkish and faded. Surreal. Snipes twitched. His eyes rolled back into his head. His body seized.

Sometimes violence is the only option. Even now, in defense of my life, in the defense of the lives of those I love, I would not hesitate to use force if that was the only option I had. But now I have a deeper understanding of my relationship with violence. It's rooted in fear, manifested in anger. I lose my ability to think, to rationalize. I lose the ability to process better options. I lose my morals. Myself. I've lost myself. When pushed to a certain point, when anger becomes too much to contain, I need the release. Deep down I enjoy the release. That's what scares me. I don't want to lose myself. That day in Southern California I lost myself. I stalked forward, cocked back my leverage, and sent my dusty black boot into Snipes' small-town Texas head.

Then they were on me. Pounds and pounds of camouflaged men, their knees, their elbows, their forearms pressing me into the earth. I don't remember who tackled me or how many people it took to restrain me, but I do remember not being allowed to eat my first meal of Marine Corps boot camp.

They put me in shackles. I was handcuffed by the ankles and wrists in a medieval-looking contraption involving a smooth and chipped wooden board with holes and chains. A light drizzle came down as I stood with my back to the platoon, all present and in formation, besides Snipes, who had been carted off on a stretcher and stuffed into an ambulance. The drizzle cooled my hot skin. I closed my eyes and thought of the song by Tony! Toni! Toné!: It Never Rains in Southern California. Raphael Saadiq singing about catching a flight, missing some girl. It never rains in Southern California, he sang. Raphael Saadiq lied. I hadn't even been in Southern California a week and it was already raining.

Hollywood couldn't have drawn up the scene any better. The rain falling. The irony. I won't pretend to remember what was going through my head in that moment, but I do remember not knowing if Snipes was dead or alive. I do remember thinking my own life as I knew it was over.

After not getting any D-I scholarship offers, I'd joined the Marines on the pretense of playing for the All Marine's basketball team. A team that didn't actually exist, at least not in the capacity that my recruiter described it. He told me I'd have a regular job, an admin job, but if I made the team—of course I would make the team—my real job would be to represent my country on the basketball court, travelling overseas. He sold me on the G.I. Bill. Told me I'd only be twenty-three when my four years were over. That I'd be able to play D-I ball then. I looked at my other options: Ferris State University or Muskegon Community College, and chose the Marines. I signed my name on the dotted line.

I wonder what I was thinking about as I stood there in those shackles, the drizzle pelting my camouflage cap. Was I thinking about all the hours I'd invested in the concrete. Those lonely hours spent in the hot summer, covered in sweat. Jumper after jumper. Perfecting my game. Those Michigan

winters. The bitter cold. Shoveling a foot of snow off the driveway. Shooting with ungloved hands. The flick of the wrist. The crunch of the net. The
thud of the ball on frozen cement. I was always, always, practicing.

I wonder if I suspected my hoop dreams had already failed. I was a
good, but not great high school basketball player. I could jump out the gym,
handle the rock, and drain it from anywhere on the court. If I were 6'5" I
would have been a menace, but I wasn't 6'5." I was only 6'0" and I couldn't
play point guard. If I played Division I, I would have been an undersized
two guard, a tweener.

At nineteen I blamed the lack of interest on my ankle. I'd sprained it at
the Mill Pond at the end of the summer and kept playing on it. It had never
fully healed by basketball season and I tweaked it again in practice. I blamed
it on a lack of exposure. The small-town stigma. My parents dragging me
out of the city and into Newaygo County. At nineteen, I did not want to
accept the truth: In spite of all those years of hard work. In spite of the
investment. I just wasn't good enough.

If I could pause one moment in my life, it would be that moment in San
Diego. I'd pause everything on that base. Everything but the rain. The rain
would be dope. Poetic. I'd want the rain in that moment. I'd want to relive
the irony my nineteen-year-old self felt that day in Southern California.

I'd snap my fingers and Recruit Abbott, age nineteen, would unpause.
He'd be baby-faced, with intense eyes. His camouflage cap would look funny
on his oddly-shaped head. He'd think he slipped into a dream. Or think it
was the hunger and the heat. He'd think he was hallucinating.

Forty-three-year-old me would be wearing a Star Wars t-shirt and cargo
shorts. R2-D2 socks and all-black Nike slides. Custom-made dog tags would
dangle over my chest. My first and last name inscribed on them. The words
Compassion, Integrity, and Loyalty below my name. I'd have a well-groomed
brown and red beard mingled with the occasional rogue gray hair. I'd be
smiling, remembering myself at that age. Before my demons had been slain.
When I was still angry at the world. When I was still emotionally immature.
Still susceptible to violence.

"I'm still dunking," I'd say. That would make him smile. "We're forty-
three and we're still dunking." He'd think about that summer before our
sophomore year at Newaygo High School, in our parent's driveway, Black
Sheep's "The Choice is Yours" playing on repeat when we tried time and

time again to throw it down. *You can get with this, or you can get with that. You can get with this, or you can get with that.* When we finally did throw it down, we looked around for a witness. Mom doing dishes, the kitchen sink just below a window overlooking the driveway. One of our siblings playing in the yard. But we were alone.

He'd size me up. See I was still in decent shape. Notice my thick shoulders and chest. The slight chub across the midsection. I know the question he'd want to ask, so I'd tell him.

"It wasn't ball," I'd say. "It was never ball."

He'd shake his head. If he wasn't cuffed he would have tugged on his ear. His cheeks would go pink. "You're a writer," I'd tell him. "You're married with eight kids. You and Razel married sisters." He'd cut me a "What the..." look when he heard about the eight kids, but then he'd notice me rocking back and forth on my feet. Favoring my left knee.

"What happened?" he'd ask.

"Nothing happened. We weren't good enough."

"The knee?"

"Arthritis. Too many hours on the concrete."

Again, he'd shake his head. "How far did we get?"

"Juco."

"Juco?"

"At twenty-three we walked on the team at Kalamazoo Valley."

"Twenty-three?"

"Twenty-three."

"What happened?"

"A lot."

"With ball?"

"Too short to play shooting guard and couldn't play the point."

"No way," he'd say. "You're killing me, man." He'd laugh that nervous laugh we still respond with sometimes when we're uncomfortable. "You're like the angel of death."

"I won't lie to you," I'd tell him. "You have a long road ahead of you, but it will all be worth it. I love my life. You'll love your life."

"We're a writer," nineteen-year-old me would say. There would be no question mark in his tone.

"That's right. We published our first novel in 2018. We're almost finished with our second one, but we set it aside to work on a book with Razel. I'm working on a book with Razel."

At that he'd smile. We've always loved Razel.

"A book about what?"

"Racism. About our shared experiences in Newaygo County and beyond."

"How long have we been married?"

"Almost five years."

"Wait, what? I thought you said we had eight kids?"

"That's a long story."

"Give me the short version."

I'd pause there. Collect my thoughts. Smell the rain. Twenty-five years later I still remember the smell of that Southern California rain. It was dirty. Wet smog. Like rain didn't actually happen often. Like that day alone made Raphael Saadiq a liar. Never is such a strong word. "You get kicked out of the Marines," I'd say, and he'd look over at the ambulance, assuming the worst. "Snipes is fine," I'd tell him. "Two weeks of bedrest and he won't remember a thing. You graduate boot camp, in fact you lead the graduation parade carrying the company guidon. But the recruiter lied to you. There is no All-Marines basketball team. Not the kind the recruiter described. You go home on leave and Dad has a heart attack. He almost dies. It shakes you to the core. You wish you were closer. Have no idea how to be closer. At forty-three we still wish we were closer. Have no idea how to be closer to Dad."

"Man."

"He's fine. He's healthy."

"Mom?"

"Looking like she's in her forties. Loving her grandkids. Healthy. Mom's great."

He'd see my expression change. He'd know. Even at age nineteen we never missed a thing. "And Ma," he'd say.

"Gone," I'd say. "A few months ago."

Recruit Abbott, age nineteen wasn't one to cry. He was one to get angry. He was one to punch brick walls, lockers, bulletin boards. Nineteen-year-old me would have shaking hands. He'd be looking at the sky. The rain would be pelting his face. He'd close his eyes. He'd take a deep breath. He wouldn't want to talk about it. He'd want to process. I'd let him. I wouldn't be there to talk about that anyway. I'd be there for the answer to a question. Not a question I would ask nineteen-year-old me. A question I ask myself now. A question I've asked myself for years.

He'd change the subject. "So, you never played pro ball, not even overseas? Not even semi-pro?"

And in that moment I would realize it didn't matter. I could tell my nineteen-year-old self the story of our life from that moment on. I could tell him about military prison. I could tell him when he got home he'd run wild, sleep around, get a stranger pregnant. I could tell him how he would feel when he first laid eyes on Keyaira, his first child. The way it changed him. Brought him to his knees. How it would make him try to make a relationship work with Keyaira's mom. I could tell him the story of how he ended up with six children, eight children. I could tell him about his first failed marriage. About divorce. About child support.

I could tell him about depression. Basketball coming to an end. Grasping for the first opportunity that came his way. Stevie in the Air Force stationed just outside of London. He was part of an independent record label looking for talent. A phone call from the owner of the record company when I was working third shift at a convenience store in Kalamazoo a few weeks after quitting the team at KVCC. "Spit," he'd say. I'd spit. A few weeks later I'd catch a flight. Record a few songs. I'd immerse myself in music. Allow myself to forget about basketball, about my first perceived failure in life.

I could tell nineteen-year-old me about the moderate success that would come after. Selling CDs out the trunk of a burgundy Delta 88. Hustling. Stevie relocating to Baltimore and meeting up with him there. Recording a song called "Carpe Diem." A song that blew up on MySpace. Would be the number one ranked song in Michigan for two weeks and be a finalist to be on the *Stomp The Yard* movie soundtrack. Yet the further I got in music, the more empty I felt. I could tell him that. The more I knew music wasn't my path. Performing for $50 a night at local bars in Grand Rapids. Selling a few CDs. Out until 2 a.m. and have to go to work the next morning.

I could tell nineteen-year-old me about the night I quit music. Sitting at a bar on the Northeast side late at night waiting to perform. Smoking a Black

N Mild. Looking around. An audience of maybe seventy-five people. A CD full of songs that weren't me. Feeling like a sellout. The project funded by a friend. The pressure to conform to the status quo. To create club songs. I could tell nineteen-year-old me about that feeling of confinement. Trapped in someone else's life. Someone else's words. Not knowing it was words all along. Not knowing how close I actually was to the path I'm on now. That three sixteen-bar verses just wasn't enough space to get the words out. I needed more space.

I could tell nineteen-year-old me about moving into Denny's basement. Carpeted but cold. A king-sized mattress that sat atop a box spring with no frame. Six kids every-other weekend, Christmas Break, Spring Break, and the last three weeks of the summer. I could tell him about rock bottom. Beyond rock bottom. Rock ceilinged. Rock floored. Rock walled. Nowhere to go at all. A slab in every direction. Imprisoned. Friends and family whispering about me. Talking behind my back. My children packed into that tight space.

I could tell nineteen-year-old me about being unemployed. Applying to hundreds of jobs after getting downsized from a salaried position. Going on twenty interviews. Five years of administrative experience in higher education, but only an associate's degree. Everyone required a bachelor's degree.

I could tell nineteen-year-old me Denny's sad story. How he was going through hard times too. Also a single father. Denny had custody of his daughter Dennia and his son Kymen. His own dreams fading. Losing his football scholarship and his freedom after getting arrested for possession of cocaine and an unregistered firearm. He'd been named the GLIAC Rookie of the Year shortly before getting in trouble. A tremendous talent. Denny should have been playing on Sundays. He should have been returning punts and coming across the middle. He was pound for pound the most freakish athlete I've ever known. He is pound for pound the strongest man I've ever known. An alien.

I could tell nineteen-year-old me Denny's success story. The way he kept his nose clean after his children were born. Starting a construction company from the ground up. Owning a home in his twenties. How he was flourishing before the housing market crashed in 2008. Could tell him how neither me nor Denny quit when things got bad, then worse. For those three years that I lived in his basement we were in it together. Just like we were in it together back on Tulip Street in White Cloud. All my bridges burned. The whispers behind my back. My little big brother was the only one who believed in me. The son of Diane Cartwright through and through. Denny is his mother's son.

I could tell nineteen-year-old me about our journey to writing. About the night I stumbled across my future shortly after moving into that basement. Pacing. Drinking a twenty-four ounce Steel Reserve. A beer that tastes like vodka and piss. Trying to numb my way to sleep. My sons Kevin and Simeon knocked out on the couch. My daughters Keyaira, Van, Andi, and Lauren sleeping together on that king-sized mattress. I'll never forget how I felt in that moment; coming to the realization that my life was my fault, accepting the blame. Understanding that I had a long road ahead. That undoing the damage would take some time.

I could tell nineteen-year-old me about sitting down at the computer that night. Clicking on Grand Valley State University's website and searching majors. Discovering they had a Writing program. I could tell him how I would go on to get my degree at GVSU. Go on to earn an MFA in Fiction from the Vermont College of Fine Arts. Publish short stories in reputable journals. Publish my first novel.

I could tell nineteen-year-old me about Vanessa. How I'd meet her at a crossroad in my life. One foot in the past. One foot in the future. On the edge of becoming me. The real me. The me who had spent his life wrestling with God, done wrestling and ready to listen. I could tell him about our wedding at Rosa Parks Circle. Our reception at the B.O.B. in downtown Grand Rapids. Our honeymoon in Costa Rica. I could tell him about Jude and Jackie, the children I'd be gifted in my forties. Gifted. I'd spent most of my fatherhood missing my children. Every-other-weekend was never enough. Isn't enough. I never stop missing my children. How I never planned on having more kids before I met Vanessa, but I'm happy I did. To wake up everyday to your family is a blessing. And though it doesn't make up for all of those years missing my older kids, it gives me the opportunity to be the kind of father I was not allowed to be to my older children. I am blessed.

I could tell nineteen-year-old me about the events that led to me and Razel writing this book. About the execution of Ahmaud Arbery. The execution of George Floyd. I could tell him what it's been like raising biracial children. Being married to a black wife. I could remind him of his time in

Newaygo. I could open those wounds. I could tell him things to prepare him for the racism he will encounter in the coming years.

I could tell nineteen-year-old me the true story of his life and he wouldn't believe me. Recruit Abbott, age nineteen had a hard head. Recruit Abbott, age nineteen was invincible. Recruit Abbott, age nineteen was so blinded by his own ambition that he didn't know his own limitations.

But I wouldn't tell him. I have the answer to my question. I wouldn't tell him about the brig, the babies, the divorce, the hardship. None of it. Each step brought me to where I am now. My history doesn't define me; it created me. Led me to Vanessa, who I never saw coming, who challenges me always to be the best version of myself. Recruit Abbott, age nineteen did not deserve Vanessa. Doesn't even deserve the story of Vanessa. Would run full speed in the opposite direction of Vanessa. That Daniel was a boy; he wasn't a man.

Daniel Abbott, age forty-three, is a husband, a father, and a writer. He is a child of God. Recruit Abbott age nineteen would not respect that. Recruit Abbott, age nineteen had his own image of the ideal life: a perma-bachelor living in a skyrise above a city, women coming and going, the kind of disposable income that would allow him to travel on a whim, point to a random place on a map and cop a plane ticket. No responsibility but himself. Nothing tying him down.

Recruit Abbott, age nineteen did not have the capacity to understand the substance of marriage. The bond struggle builds. The feeling of having someone support you through that struggle and fight with you through that struggle the way Vanessa fights with me. He couldn't comprehend the joy of fatherhood. The sacrifice you make for your children. The way self gets pushed aside. The way you show up for everything: football games, basketball games, those excruciating multi-school choir/orchestra/band events where your child is only on stage for five minutes, but you have to stay for three hours. Recruit Abbott, age nineteen did not have the capacity to understand love.

I have the answer to my question. I think I've had the answer all along.

Recruit Abbott, age nineteen would get us kicked out of the Marines. He'd spend two months in military prison. He'd go on to get a stranger pregnant. Have six kids playing house. He'd go to jail for child support. He'd pursue a career as a hip-hop artist and have moderate success. Eventually he'd find his path. He'd find his purpose. His wife. His career.

I have the answer to my question.

I'd taste that Southern California rain and think about that Tony! Toni! Toné! song. I'd look at the me I was and take pride in the me I had become. I'd appreciate the nineteen-year-old me's recklessness. He gave me Keyaira, Kevin, Simeon, Savanna, Andi, and Lauren. He gave me life experience. He gave me something to write about.

I have the answer to my question.

That answer…

I wouldn't change a thing.

I Fit the Description

RAZEL JONES
KENTWOOD, MICHIGAN 2014

That day at the park I was looking forward to spending time with my daughter. She was a year and a half old then. That day we had time to adventure together, as Camille met with a group of leaders from our church for some brainstorming and event planning at Pinewood Park, a normally quiet park in the Grand Rapids suburb, Kentwood.

Having just over eight months experience taking steps with those new feet, the park was an amazing place for Kayden to try out her newly-found skills. The slide was overwhelming, because of its uncontrollable nature: the height, the speed, the unknown destination, the separation from Daddy. She explored each area of the park with curiosity, before time-and-time again returning to her excursion of choice—the baby swing—which I was more than willing to push as long as the action maintained her peaceful contentment and joy. As she swung up and down she attentively consumed the sights from the various elevations afforded by a strong push from her personal joy-enabler for the afternoon, better known as "Da'yee." How I miss being called that sweet name.

When Kayden and I returned to the group, they were working diligently on laptops. Camille led them as they sat at picnic tables. Camille and I had been married for ten years, and although her skills and abilities merit the forefront, she has always preferred the background. I watched that day as she led the group with her keen organizational skills, planning events that would make me and my vision for the church look, and be better.

Jessica Ganzie was with us, a newlywed of two months. We had somehow pulled her away from her husband, Darius, for the meeting. She and Darius were both proudly from the D, Detroit city. They had joined the church while students at Ferris State. Recent graduates with new careers, they were assets to our team for sure. They'd remained with us even after moving the sixty miles south to Kentwood.

Though we were nearly fifty years after the burnings of black churches in Alabama and Georgia, we were only a few years after the vandalism of a black church in Crane, Texas at the hands of a white man seeking entry into the Aryan Brotherhood. We were just a couple years after the burning of a black church in Springfield, Massachusetts in response to Barack Obama's presidential victory. History repeats itself; racism repeats itself. Darius had committed himself to making sure the church was safe and making sure I was safe. He monitored who entered and exited the building and who accessed my office; he arrived at each service in advance of me and wouldn't exit until I did. He was constantly asking to carry a gun for security. It's a good thing he wasn't there that day.

Anita was with us in the park. She had come through the White Cloud school system about ten years behind me. We attended the same church growing up, and she became my niece by marriage. Anita joined Victory Life about two years after it began.

Tracey rounded out the planning group. Tracey was the church's executive assistant and sang on the praise team with her younger sister Vanessa, and older sister Camille. One thing about Tracey is she loves hard and believes in defending those she loves. She had just given birth to her second child, Cayleb, who was also present that day, and was just two-and-a-half months old. Vulnerable.

We would soon find that we were all vulnerable.

Even at a great distance, I spotted the officers and knew they were headed in our direction. I think it's an innate defense mechanism, especially for black men, to be aware of the presence of police. You can breathe in their presence, like the smell of a gas leak, alerting the senses that danger is near. *Be still. Be alert. Be aware. Be cool.* Your mind prepares for the possible explosion, while your body remains still, unlike the response in the room that smells of gas, where at least you have the option and responsibility to run like hell.

I couldn't run that time. I had to protect the group. As they came closer, I could see Jessica's demeanor change. She had spotted them too. Her head turned to the side, and her lower cheek curled up. On her exhale, she quietly questioned, "Now, what do they want?"

My gaze shifted to Camille. Camille's eyes shifted to Kayden, and to Tracey, who clinched her newborn son a little tighter. Anita was silent. We all braced for impact.

They had their hands on their weapons as they approached. My heart raced faster than normal; my imagination displayed visions of the worst-possible scenario. But, I had to...*Be still. Be alert. Be aware. Be cool.*

I forced a look of calm onto my face for the sake of the group. *If I'm calm, they'll feel calm,* was my thought. My look was a front. I wasn't calm. My eyes locked back on the weapons. What could they possibly want? *Be still. Be alert. Be aware. Be cool.*

I could recognize the look in the lead officer's eyes. It reminded me of the cop on Lester Street in White Cloud. I was his target. I didn't know why, but he was focused on me, just as I was honing in on him. The other officer was his accompanist. He marched to the cadence of a non-rhythmic drum. He moved closer slower, while my heart beat faster.

My heart beat, beat, beat. His feet stepped. Beat, beat, beat, step. The triplet of my heartbeat to his steps formed the soundtrack of the experience. For just a moment, it was as if no one else existed. Like a showdown in the Wild West, but only he had a weapon. The lead officer and I were out of alignment, out of syncopation—I was out of time. They were upon me. Upon us. I told myself one more time.

Be still. Be alert. Be aware. Be cool.

Keeping my cool included watching my tone. Adjusting my intonation. Preparing my words before allowing them to enter that tense atmosphere. I was doing my best to prepare the perfect address for this imperfect situation. One final thought entered my mind. *Say something early in the encounter in an intelligent way so that he knows the caliber of the person he's talking to. Show him you're different.*

I'm definitely different. I'm not different. Which is it? Maybe it's both.

Inside my head, my thoughts screamed. *Why am I in this situation? Why are we in this situation? I make choices to never be in this situation. Yet, here I am. Again.* Walking down Lester Street again. Being pulled over by the Grand Valley Campus Police after doing nothing wrong again. Being assumed to be a criminal again. Being questioned about activities I wasn't involved in again. Being watched more closely than my white friends again. Being followed around the store again. Being mistaken for a suspect again.

No more time to plan. The plan was incomplete. *Scrap the plan. Just act natural.*

Be still. Be alert. Be aware. Be cool.

I shifted my conversation to the armed approacher, "What's up?" I asked.

"We received a call and we're looking for someone here in the park. Can I see your ID?"

My focus was split between the question he asked, the thoughts running through my head, and my constant awareness that neither of their hands had departed from their weapons. They were standing next to the center of my world, Camille and Kayden. It's tough to answer questions appropriately when you're innocent and unarmed and engaged in an unwanted scenario with a stranger with a gun.

There I sat—the only black man in proximity, at a table with four black women, and two black babies. There we sat, just a few weeks after the tragedies in Ferguson, Missouri where eighteen-year-old, Michael Brown, Jr. was killed by Officer Darren Wilson. A witness in that case stated that the young man had raised his hands and shouted, "Don't shoot," but Officer Wilson reportedly fired his weapon twelve times, hitting Brown with six bullets before his request and blood flowed out of his battered body, leading to the death of his body and his dreams. He would never enroll in college. Never propose to his soul mate. Never celebrate an anniversary. Never open a business. Never pursue a career. Never purchase a home. Never have the opportunity to push his little girl on a swing. Officer Wilson was not indicted on any charges. Earlier that week, I had just spoken to a group of students, staff, faculty, and community leaders in response to the Michael Brown shooting, at a prayer vigil. Would I be next?

My eyes shifted off the weapon and onto the face of Camille. *Please don't say anything, Camille,* I thought. When you've been married to someone for a long time, you can speak without words. All it takes is a look. Ten years isn't a huge amount of time, but it was long enough to have developed our *eye language*. Her look communicated a desire to clarify why they clung to their weapons.

I responded with my eyes, *Be still. Be alert. Be aware. Be cool.* I didn't want the attention that was focused on me to shift to her. I knew she had the tendency to speak her mind without fear—with an expectation that the other party would have to hear her logic. When in an unfair, and seemingly uncontrollable position, the emotion that overtakes Camille is not fear, it's rage. Yet, she was forced to sit with the same helplessness I felt as we were not in a position of authority in that situation. We had to comply even though we knew the officers were wasting their time and ours. We had done nothing wrong. We were minding our business. Minding God's business.

I glanced at the gun, then back to Camille, who was now holding Kayden securely in her arms. Even the baby recognized the tension of our predicament. She needed comfort to endure the unnecessary experience as she wiggled in Camille's arms, wishing to get down and roam. It was one thing for me to be threatened, but at that moment my family was threatened. Endangered. I wanted to take Kayden, grab Camille by the hand, and lead the group out of the situation. My heart was beating fast, but it wasn't the beat of fear. It was the beat of frustration—frustrated to be treated like a criminal when no crime had occurred. I wanted to take control of the situation. But, I couldn't. Couldn't take the chance of things going wrong. Couldn't make this worse for Camille and Kayden. Couldn't put Tracey and Cayleb in a worse spot. Couldn't escalate the situation and lose my cool in front of Jessica and Anita.

Would Camille, Kayden, and those loyal vision actualizers who had already beaten the odds in their own lives now have their lives changed for the worse? Jessica had basically raised herself, overcame family challenges, and pushed her way through college. Anita was raised in a single-parent home, overcame the racism of White Cloud, and moved to a more diverse place— but, that diversity didn't change the outcome in that situation. Tracey was a young mother who didn't stop; she completed community college, then her Bachelor's degree at Grand Valley, started her career, and bought a home, overcoming challenge after challenge.

They were fighters; they were overcomers, but each sat in stillness with helplessness and tension as this scenario unfolded. Was there anything I could do to deescalate the situation to ensure the group's safety? I couldn't deescalate the situation, because I wasn't in control of the situation. The anger came back in the middle of the introspection causing hopefulness to exit the scenario, leaving me with only expectation based on commonality of experience. Expectation that something was going to go wrong, even though we had done nothing wrong.

They kept touching their weapons.

My eyes made contact with the bright brown eyes of Kayden. She was watching my every move. Then Camille. Then Jessica. Then Anita. Then Tracey. All of their eyes were on me. They would respond how I responded. That is the weight of leadership. The duty of connection. My actions didn't only impact me.

I knew my best option was to comply. I needed to get the situation over with. I reached for my license. I held my tongue…but it felt heavy. This guy had no care for how this situation was impacting my loved ones. His hand had not moved from his weapon, which was obviously his source of courage. At that moment, I noticed his partner had relaxed his hand. He let it hang loosely at his side, no longer on his weapon. That, along with the hesitant look in his eyes let me know he was not completely on-board with his partner's actions any longer…yet, he appeared to have the privileged right to remain silent. He was complicit, but silence was no longer working for me. I once again attempted to tell myself, *Be still. Be alert. Be aware*…Wait, there was one more part, but I had lost the rhythm.

One-by-one, I saw anxiety deepening on the faces of those with me. The anger was growing, frustration was mounting, and negativity was brewing. The women with me were all fighters. Overcomers. No two men, even with weapons and badges could've outmatched our spirited crew. Not one of us was the type to let injustice go.

Breathe! Get yourself together, Razel. I couldn't afford to let my mouth make the situation go further and last longer than it had to. I knew it could end poorly. *Be an example. You're a husband. You're a father. You're a pastor. They're watching you.*

The voice in my head changed to a more facetious tone, *Be a good boy, Razel… Boy? That's probably a term he would have liked to call me. That's how he viewed me. I'm no boy; I'm a man*…I know he didn't say it, but sometimes words can be seen, even when they aren't said. He thought it. I felt it. He felt powerful directing my actions. He felt strong being in control of the situation. He felt dominant because we were forced to listen. I had to say something.

"So, I fit the description, huh?"

He quickly looked up into my eyes. He saw a man who knew he had done nothing wrong. The officer abruptly responded, "Yes, you do…"

One of two things was true about his readiness for my question: He was waiting for that question—anticipating that I would distrust the sincerity of his premise for engaging me, or he had played this game before with some other black man who felt the need, as I had, to question his intent. I knew at that moment that if a description did exist, the only guaranteed match between me and the description was, black man.

I provided my ID. His left hand reached to accept my proof of freedom. Like a freedman during the days of slavery, revisiting the South for the first time, I cautiously handed my papers over to the authority, hoping that he wouldn't corrupt my incorruptible life, liberty, and pursuit of happiness. While his left hand accepted my proof, his right hand remained postured in ready-position to lift the gun if he felt the slightest discomfort.

The officers soon came to the realization that I knew all along—I was not who they were looking for. There was no apology. No recognition of the application of stereotype. No remorse for ruining a beautiful day. Simply a "You're all set; have a nice day..." No explanation to us. I still have no idea how information from my license could've proven that I wasn't the suspect.

At that moment Camille communicated through that shared language of a look as she motioned with her eyes to another group at the park that was watching from about twenty-five feet away. A white woman with her children was the probable description provider. She called the police on me. There was no way for us to know that for sure, but we had agreement on the strong possibility. For what? What had I done? Why did she feel threatened by my presence—by our presence? I hadn't had a thought about her, but as the officers left our group, walking into this white woman's space, it was clear that the explanation that was owed to me was being given to this informant of nothingness. Right in front of my eyes, the officers were having an inaudible conversation with this woman. What happened to their search for a suspect? If everyone in the area was threatened due to a suspicious report, why stop and have a chat before continuing the manhunt? Go find my twin. No, they'd found who they wanted to find. I am convinced they had responded to this woman's call.

That day, the white woman was equivalent to the white woman described as *Central Park Karen*, who called 911 on an innocent black man, fictionalizing a story to portray him as threatening when he was really just birdwatching. She was the white woman known as *Permit Patty*, made famous for calling the police on an eight-year-old black girl who sold water in a park in San Francisco. The accuser complained that the little girl had no permit to sell the water. She was the white woman nicknamed *BBQ Betty*, who called the police on a black family, for simply barbecuing at a local park in Oakland. None of these black people had done anything wrong either. None of these white people cared.

That call could have been my death sentence. She trusted that the police would handle the situation appropriately…only there was no situation. The whole thing was unnecessary.

Should we report the incident to the police department? What will that do? Will it even matter? Why waste my time? Shortly thereafter, we left the park. On our way out, in the distance we saw that the patrol had continued—the harassment continued. The officers were making their way to a small group of black adolescents minding their business, hooping, in another part of the park. I should've stayed to make sure no injustice happened to them, but I didn't have anything left. Exhausted, my energy had all been expended trying my hardest to…*Be still. Be alert. Be aware. Be cool.* Fatigued from carrying the weight of being black. An undeserved burden for such a beautiful existence.

My thoughts turned to my baby. She started the day exploring the park, befriended the swing. She had an unblemished belief in the goodness of humanity. Would that day be the subconscious beginning of the end of her hope? Would the faint, distant memory of that experience give her an unexplainable, natural—but not-so-natural—learned disbelief in the goodness and decency of law enforcement? I hoped not, yet I hoped so. I need her to be respectful, yet cautious. I need her to live. I need her to do a better job than me of holding her heavy tongue. I will not be able to be with her during every encounter she has with the police—every encounter she has with racism. I need things to change for her, just as my parents, grandparents, great-grandparents, and beyond needed things to change for each generation that followed them. But it has not changed…enough. It has not changed enough when my innocence still isn't enough to shield me from experiences that whiteness would completely prevent. It has not changed enough because the oppression has not stopped.

Don't get me wrong, a lot has changed…lynchings have become white knees pressed against a black neck. Black knees in kneepads, in protest on the ground have become career enders for Super Bowl-contending quarterbacks. Attempting to spend a counterfeit twenty-dollar bill has become guilty before investigation—a death sentence without a trial—a public execution. Looking at a construction site has become justification for chasing, harassing, fighting, shooting, and killing a man…a man…amen. I agree with myself, as I have to do because whiteness often doesn't allow itself to agree with my truth. We tell you we're hurting. You tell us we're not. I hurt. I said, I hurt! When will this country ever begin to believe me?

Did I look dangerous as I sat at a picnic table with church leaders? Did I look like a criminal when I was pushing my daughter on the baby swing? Did this onlooking white woman's suspicion merit calling the police? Did their suspicion merit approaching our group, our parishioners, my wife, our babies, with hands on lethal weapons? How did I fit the description? What was described? What crime had been committed? If I called the police on her, would the same protocol have been followed? Simple answer. Tell the truth.

Unfortunately, the truth is that in the eyes of many, in and out of law enforcement, as a black man, I am seen as threatening, dangerous, and criminal. Still to others, I am not seen as a man at all, but instead an animal—3/5 of a man. This is evident as we see black people being killed by police, and *concerned citizens* standing their ground, defending themselves from crimes that never occurred and attacks that never happened. Self-defense? When you have a gun, pepper spray, a billy club, a taser, a partner, fists, handcuffs, and training, why must you kill them? That's not self-defense, that's privilege. That's genocide. It's done because the system says it can be done.

So, we are left with the haunting images and stories of the modern day lynchings of:

Eric Garner
July 17, 2014 "I can't breathe."

Michael Brown, Jr.
August 9, 2014 "Hands up, don't shoot."

Tamir Rice
November 22, 2014 Playing with a toy gun at twelve years old.

Natasha McKenna
February 8, 2015. Tased to death in police custody.

Walter Scott
April 4, 2015. Traffic stop involving a defective light on a vehicle.

Sandra Bland
July 12, 2015. Traffic stop.Found hanged in a jail cell three days after being arrested during a traffic stop and harshly confronted by an arresting officer. Her death was ruled a suicide.

Alton Sterling
July 5, 2016. Selling CDs.

Philando Castile
July 6, 2016. Reaching for his license while his young daughter watched tried to comfort her father from the back seat.

Stephon Clark
March 18, 2018. Believed to be armed—no weapon found.

Breonna Taylor
March 13, 2020 (shot eight times in her home in a   in a drug raid where plain-clothed police entered the wrong address with a no-knock warrant.

Ahmaud Arbery
February 23, 2020. Jogging while black.

George Floyd
May 25, 2020. "I can't breathe." Again.

Within the last six years these, and many more, were executed with no trial. These black women and men did not need to die. They did not have to die.

In the U.S. Constitution, which was designed to bring order and law to our nation, my slave ancestors were counted as just 3/5 of a person, leaving

2/5 of our identity unstated and undefined, but not human. When one is treated less than human by the legal documents of the country, is it a surprise that there is a reduced allegiance to the flag of that country, and at times, a reduced pride in being a citizen of the country? This patriotic emblem is the symbol, for which many African Americans have fought and died, yet the sacrifice was, and is, for a country that has not upheld the positive promises made to its citizens in that same document, as it relates to black people. Inhumane treatment directed to people of color is a recurring theme in the history of my country. Our country.

It is this perspective of black people as less than human, held by far too many individuals, that has enabled inhumane murders at the hands of people filled with contempt and disgust for an entire race of people. This is what allowed Officer Derek Chauvin to pin George Floyd to the ground, facedown, while handcuffed for over eight minutes, with his knee and body weight lethally pressed on Mr. Floyd's neck…for more than eight minutes…eight minutes… In that time, as Mr. Floyd begged for his life and exclaimed his inability to breathe, Chauvin did not think of Mr. Floyd as a human being. Had he thought that this man may have a family who loves him, is someone's son, has hopes and aspirations, could be dealing with challenges beyond his control, is a father…God created him—he has dreams—he has a story…If Mr. Floyd was viewed as a human being, I do not believe his life would've ended in this horrific manner.

I dare not parallel my experience with the police to the experiences of the many deceased black women and men who have been murdered at the hands of white authority figures. Their lives ended, while mine has continued. I do believe the same perspective was present in all of these situations. On that day, in their eyes I wasn't a pastor; I wasn't an author; I wasn't a Christian; I wasn't a husband; I wasn't a father; I wasn't a son; I wasn't a human resources professional; I wasn't a professional communicator; I wasn't an American; I wasn't a college graduate; I wasn't a taxpayer; I wasn't a business owner. Honestly, I probably wasn't even a human…I was, at best, a suspect—more likely, a criminal.

I could have been killed. Kayden could have lost her daddy. Camille could have lost her husband. A congregation could have lost its pastor.

So, if the description presented is, "betrayed man who through education and experience has been lulled into believing the lie that the provisions of protection, justice, reward for hard work, and equal opportunity are intended for him,"—or, "dark-skinned man who is misjudged, prejudged, falsely judged, and assumed guilty, even if proven innocent,"—or, "society-contributing man who is asked to run a mile-long race in which the competition is given a two-lap head-start and then when beaten, told that he should have pulled himself up by his bootstraps so he could win the race,"—or, "hardworking man who does all he can to achieve a good quality of life for his family, while being mistreated, overlooked, suspected, and accused of only finding success because of the alleged handouts this country has given him,"—or, "black man who is seen as less than by those with supremacist outlooks and a view of black people as 3/5 (or less) human...," if that's the narrative, then unfortunately...

I fit the description.

Forfeiting White Privilege

DANIEL ABBOTT
NEWAYGO, MICHIGAN CIRCA 2007

I was at odds with God back then and I'm certain He was at odds with me. Weary of watching me claw at doors that were better left closed. Weary of watching me dig holes and toss myself into them. Weary of watching me struggle against His will, trying to impose my own. I suspect God was just tired. Of me. Of the Daniel Abbott who limped out of his twenties and into his thirties. Knowing I was destined for greater than the life I was living. Too hard-headed to listen to that still, small voice that likes to whisper in my bones. So God slipped away and watched me from a distance.

He watched me.

I was a couple years removed from going to jail for child support. After my children's mom and I separated, we had agreed to a 50/50 parenting time split, but the Kent County Friend of the Court didn't seem to care. I was walloped to the tune of $1,500 a month, a sum I couldn't come close to paying. The arrears piled up while I saved every receipt for groceries, clothes, entertainment—any expense related to my children.

A court date was scheduled and I showed up in a suit I probably borrowed from Denny. Which means the pants were flooding and the jacket was too loose in the shoulders. My head would've been shaved clean. A lined beard. Joop cologne. I was armed with a black three-ringed binder full of receipts. So naive. I believed the proof was in that binder. That justice would prevail. I went in feeling self-righteous, making the poor assumption that I was dealing with human beings and not paper-pushers. Assuming I'd be treated like a human being and not a case number. Assuming that the truth, that I was providing at least 50 percent of my children's needs, would clear my name.

What occurred that day was like that scene in the first *Matrix* movie, when Neo's mouth was sealed shut by the voodoo of Agent Smith. The social worker spewed monotone jargon while he sipped coffee from a paper cup. A skinny, disinterested black man, probably tired of his caseload. He wouldn't even look at the receipts when I opened the binder and slid it in front of him. "Those receipts could be for anything," he said. Sip. Sip. A bite of his donut. "You need to pay $3,000 or you're going in front of the judge." He finally looked me in the eyes. He was bored. My life was a mere slice of his day, a portion of his overworked, underpaid career of punishing present fathers for the crimes of deadbeat dads.

When I went in front of the judge she didn't want my story either. $3,000 or I was going to jail, she told me. Moments later I was escorted away in handcuffs.

Those days it was a fight being a father. My first wife and I got married with good intentions, but we both came out with wounds. I have no regrets. My kids love their mother. I respect their mother. The fight in her. The sacrifices she's made for our children. My problem with her in the past was that I'd been the one on the receiving end of her blows. I imagine she feels that she was on the receiving end of mine. My wounds have healed. All is forgiven on my part. And I pray she's found the same peace as me.

Shortly after being released from the Kent County jail I moved into a small studio apartment in the Heritage Hill area of Grand Rapids. I had four children at the time: Keyaira, Kevin, Simeon, and Savanna. We spent our first couple weekends cramped in that tiny apartment before I decided to bring the kids to my parents' house in Newaygo during my parenting time. We'd pack into an old, red Mercury Cougar and make that forty-five minute drive up M-37 on Friday evening and then back down again on Sunday when I returned the kids to their mother.

Keyaira must have been nine at the time, which would have made the boys seven and six. Would have made Van five. Four biracial kids squeezed into a beat-up Cougar. Making that trip to racially homogenous Newaygo. During those debilitating child support days I always rode dirty. I'd buy car insurance to get a plate and then I'd stop paying my monthly bill. After my birthday would come and go, and my plate would expire, I'd continue driving. Continue picking up my kids and making that trip to Newaygo.

On one of those Fridays we entered Newaygo and avoided a stoplight by taking a side-street just past Speedway. The short cut led to M-82 where we'd hook a right, and then another right down the street where my parents have lived since we moved to Newaygo in 1991.

I don't remember exactly what first got that police officer's attention. When I was a young dad I had energy. We had fun. I might have been blasting Lupe Fiasco's *The Cool* album and singing "Go Baby!" with the windows down. That's feasible. Innocent. For certain we were innocent. We were smiling. All of us. Me. My four biracial children. My two biracial suns. My two biracial moons. Innocent. Guilty of nothing but being brown in Newaygo.

The cop was standing outside of his patrol car talking to his friend, an off-duty cop who lived on that street. I knew he was an off-duty cop because everybody knows everybody in Newaygo. Because you could see his house through the thin woods between my parents' house and his, and my dad once pointed to his house and told me the man was a cop shortly after he moved in. The on-duty cop glanced our way. He was too far away to see that my license plate was expired.

There was no way he could've seen if a taillight was out.

I didn't have a taillight out.

From my rearview mirror I watched him rush to his patrol car. I heard his sirens chirp. Saw his lights go on. I thought about my expired plate. I thought about my canceled insurance. Thought about how I couldn't afford to pay either ticket. Then I thought about the look on the cop's face when he saw my children. The way he rushed to his cruiser.

When I think of that day I'm reminded of the summer of 1991 when we moved to Newaygo. My parents had brought me to a gathering with some of their friends in Croton, on the edge of Newaygo and White Cloud. That's where I met LaLa. He was shooting alone on a dirt basketball court with a janky rim and a half-chewed net. He was a few years older than me. The only black face at the white gathering. Only he wasn't really at the gathering. He was there to ball. I had been dragged to the gathering. The only thing I wanted to do was ball.

We connected that day and exchanged numbers. In the weeks that followed, he occasionally picked me up in his blue Ford Escort and rescued me from my parent's driveway, where I spent most of that summer, and most of my time in Newaygo, shooting alone, or doing drills with my brother

Brian, who is six years younger than me. LaLa was the first person in Newaygo County besides my kid-brother, Brian, to treat me like a friend.

LaLa had a disease called Chronic Granulomatous. His body didn't produce enough white blood cells to kill off bacteria. The disease deteriorated part of his spine. He'd had multiple surgeries by the time I met him and he had to wear a back brace. He'd die young, just a few years after that summer, from complications during a viscous bout with pneumonia.

I remember one of those times LaLa picked me up. I'm not sure where we were going. Perhaps to hoop. Perhaps to just drive around. I don't remember who was with him that particular day. We got pulled over just past the bridge leaving Newaygo. We were making a left toward Fremont. I was the only white kid in the car. We were all boys. One white boy and three black boys. The black boys lay face down on the concrete that day. Their hands cuffed behind their backs. The lone white boy sat on the edge of the road watching. I was uncuffed. Conflicted. Fourteen. Wishing I was cuffed face down on the concrete with my friends. Relieved I wasn't cuffed face down on the concrete with my friends.

There were two cops. Both white. Both male. No reason was given for why we were pulled over. No reason was given for why my friends were cuffed. Why I wasn't. They didn't care about LaLa's spine. LaLa showed no pain, though I know it must have hurt him. He wouldn't give those racist cops the satisfaction. Cars slowed down as they passed. White drivers with white passengers. White parents and their white children, watching. Not seeing, I imagine, three innocent black boys being harassed by racist police officers. Seeing three black criminals being brought to justice. Young minds being shaped into wrong thinking. Generational ignorance being reinforced through misconstrued observation.

What I remember most about LaLa was his infectious smile.

When we were allowed to go, when we climbed back into his car, LaLa wasn't smiling. He was stoic. A kid reminded that he was black in Newaygo County. Reminded he was black in America. No one spoke. Maybe the radio was on. Maybe a tape was in the tape deck, I don't remember. What I remember is silence. What I remember is feeling guilty. Guilty of my skin. I remember feeling powerless. I remember some other nameless feeling. Maybe a fourteen-year-old's understanding of white privilege. I don't know. But I return to that day often. I return to that day each time another black man is murdered by the police. A black boy is murdered by the police. I return to that day every time a black American is murdered by a white American because of the color of their skin.

I remember when Treyvon Martin was murdered by George Zimmerman. The news kept showing this black and white photo of him in a hoodie. I stared at the picture so long one night that it felt like he was speaking to me from the grave. "How could you let them do this to me?" he asked me. Them. There is a them. The George Zimmermans of the world. The Derrick Chauvins. The Greggory and Travis McMichaels.

I have seen racial inequality firsthand and I have been silent.

I will no longer be silent.

When I think of that day with LaLa, I remember the way those cops separated us. I received their message: You're safe. They are not safe. I doubt I was thinking about LaLa, though, that day when the cop pulled up behind me in my parents' driveway and I told my children to go into the house. My four biracial children. My two biracial suns. My two biracial moons. Innocent. Guilty of nothing but being brown in Newaygo. I wasn't thinking about Black Lives Matter. I wasn't thinking about racial injustice. I wasn't thinking about police brutality. I was thinking about me. I was thinking, how dare you pull me over when I did nothing wrong. How dare you pull me over because I have biracial children.

"Stay in the car," the officer told my kids.

"Why'd you pull me over?" I asked.

The officer smiled. He stretched his neck in an exaggerated way and glanced at the back of the beat-up car. "Tail light," he told me. I didn't have a tail light out. He didn't mention my expired plate. I remember being angry that he didn't notice the expired plate. He'd driven behind me for almost a mile, he was trained to notice such things, and he didn't notice. I was guilty of breaking the law, but I was not being pulled over for breaking the law. I was being pulled over for breaking that age-old unspoken white law. I was tainting the precious white world that so many are fearful of losing.

The next part I don't remember. My children don't remember, only that I was angry. That I was being disrespectful. I don't remember the words, but I remember the anger. That ancient Newaygo anger. I remember gripping the door handle. I remember my dad rushing out of the house and scolding me, but I don't remember what he said. My dad has always known how to convict me with his words and his eyes. He doesn't remember what he said either. I don't know if he wants to remember what he said. I don't even remember if I was given a ticket that day. I don't remember what happened after I calmed down. My children don't remember what happened after I calmed down.

I asked each of my children who were in the car that day, all adults now, what they remembered and their answers varied. What stands out though is something Simeon told me. He remembers me losing my temper. Remembers me being disrespectful to the cop. He doesn't remember the words. But this is the part that's important. This is the reason Razel and I are writing this book. Simeon said these words and when he said them my arm hairs stood. His words were truth. His words gave me a deeper understanding of what white privilege means. I thought, really thought, because of the love I have for my wife, my children, my family, my friends, I knew what it meant to be black in America. I have the same worries as a black parent. I do. My white skin does not protect my brown-skinned children from the police. My sons and daughters will be pulled over because they are black. My sons and daughters will have to work twice as hard to get half as far because they are black. As a parent you love your children. Worry for your children. Even when they are adults. I know what it is like to be a father of black children. I do not know, truly know what it is like to be a black man in America. If I did, I would not have gripped the door handle that day and opened the car door. I would not have lost my temper.

For years I thought I was defending my children that day. I know now I was defending myself. Defending my white privilege. My, How Dare You. My right to not be harassed when I'm doing nothing wrong. The right my white skin allows me. A right I had forfeited to a certain degree by marrying black, by fathering black, by loving black. My skin does not redeem those I love. That day my skin did not redeem me. Once again I was guilty by association. What I didn't realize that day or in the years that followed was the privilege of my whiteness. How a layer of privilege was still present that day. In spite of the wrongness of what happened.

Simeon gave it to me straight. His words were truth. I learned more from my nineteen-year-old son in that moment than I had in thirty years of being immersed in black culture. Living with a black family. Being married to a black woman. Fathering black children.

Simeon's words were truth.

"Dad," he said. "I don't remember what you said to that cop." He paused.

"But if you were black you would have been shot."

Escape

RAZEL JONES
NASHVILLE, TENNESSEE 2019

The first day of the best professional job I've had. Full of excitement, nervousness, and hope. I made the one-hour commute to Nashville, Tennessee. Before making the move from Michigan, my normal commute was about fifteen minutes, and sometimes I had complained about that. But, on July 22, 2019, one hour wasn't enough time to gather my thoughts. That was the day I'd become the Director of Equity and Inclusion at Tennessee State University (TSU). It was my first time being a part of a Historically Black College or University (HBCU). My career and my life had been leading to the role. A few days before my first day of work, I received word that my oldest brother, Hendrick, Jr. was in the hospital.

In my former jobs, I'd previously worked with employee relations in HR at a Michigan college, and had been a consultant for many companies helping them do diversity-related work. My previous role was at Middle Tennessee State University, where I'd been an investigator of discrimination and harassment matters. There, I had participated in creating an institutional affirmative action plan, learning to meaningfully provide accountability, and transformation of the hiring process to ensure diverse candidates were given a fair shot in the search process. The TSU role would, for the first time, allow me to take the lead in strategizing the offerings and approach of the work. The work aimed at creating a safe environment for faculty, staff, and students to engage the experience free from harassment, discrimination, and sexual assault. I know it sounds intense to some; to me, it was a major opportunity for impact.

I continued on the highway through historic Franklin, Tennessee, I glanced to the east at the defaced statue of a confederate general on his horse. Someone had added a coat of pink paint, vandalizing the vandal who was also a

KKK leader. Doing the work of equity and inclusion in that region would be interesting.

That day would be my first time doing the work at an institution where black people were the majority. All my other positions had been at Predominantly White Institutions (PWIs). The rest of my life had been at PWIs. The TSU position would require me to think of diversity in forward and reverse.

I'd often thought about how we, black people, would be if we were the majority. If we had the power, would we become barriers to the entrance of *other* into our domain? Would we consider the value of varying perspectives? Would we be willing to let the guard down to what has historically been and open the door to what could be? It would be my turn to provide accountability to ensure that we wouldn't repeat the historic mishandling of power we had witnessed. If when given power we abuse it and perpetuate the same evils that have been inflicted on us, we have learned nothing. We have experienced pain at the hands of dominant cultures protecting their dominance. Fortifying their power. We won't repeat the cycle in reverse.

I was honored to be joining an institution that has hosted prestigious students including world-record holding Olympic champion, Wilma Rudolph; the founder and leader of Earth, Wind & Fire, Maurice White; an Alabama state senator and attorney who represented Rosa Parks in her historic civil rights case, Charles Langford; the iconic Oprah Winfrey. Politicians, athletes, inventors, entertainers, civil rights champions, world-changers, and innovators. A host of contributors who have deeply affected the African American community, and indeed the world. I'd have the opportunity to impact the impactors.

On I-65 cars advanced like worker ants sharing the road with me, attempting to arrive at the destinations of their duties. Their lane changes distracted my thoughts. Or, my thoughts distracted my driving. I'm not sure, but the thoughts prevailed.

When you have good news, you want to share it with the people you love. I had shared my excitement with my family, letting each one know of my new role. I always wanted to let Dad in on those sorts of things. After all, he sacrificed, working forty-two years at a factory so that I wouldn't have to. I owed him this kind of news. The shared lien-holder on that debt is Mom. I talked to her almost every day and knew her to be my longest-lasting supporter. Not only did she work for over twenty years in her career, she sacrificed everything to raise her children. She made a decision to focus on preparing the five of us for our journeys, leaving her educational goals as a side-note. She was our language developer and educator. Our nurse. Our chef. Our referee. Our investigator and spiritual advisor. Everything we became, she already was.

I also shared the news with my sisters. Theresa, the oldest—the trail-blazer, the Speech Pathologist. Stephanie—the supporter, the Nurse. They both have always believed in me. My older brothers were a little more complicated, but they were my superheroes. I emulated their every move. Whether Jerome's athleticism, or Hendrick, Jr.'s cooking. They both demonstrated boldness in the face of opposition. I thought, if I could be like anyone, I want to be just like them.

My oldest brother, Hendrick, Jr., marched to the beat of his own piano. A drum was not multidimensional enough to provide the cadence for Hendrick's existence. He needed high, mid, and low notes, sharps and flats, varying percussive timbre, chords and singles, octaves and scales chromatically, in all twelve keys. He needed theme music. We called him Junior. Junior liked independence. He never wanted to have to rely on anyone else. It's a Jones trait. Stubbornness and determination are two sides of the same coin.

In order to achieve this independence, Junior worked. As a teenager, at Bird's Grocery Store; then, in the early 1980s, when the first McDonalds in the county opened in Fremont, Junior began a food services career, as one of the original employees of the newly established franchise. In food services, Junior excelled. So much so, that upon graduation he decided to attend Tri-State University in Angola, Indiana to pursue culinary education. This pursuit didn't last very long. He soon found that he didn't desire to continue his collegiate career. After one semester, he returned to Michigan.

In the distance, I saw the Nashville cityscape. The buildings without distinction. I was getting closer to my destination. My first day to embark upon the next phase of my career, I thought about the conversations I had with each of my family members. They were all encouraging and excited. Each one celebrated. Well, almost each one. When I called Junior, he didn't pick up the phone.

When I think of my childhood, Junior was the kind of brother who always knew how to make me feel special. I remember way back in the early 80s when he would take me outside to play on an autumn day. The crunch of the leaves beneath my young feet intensified as we ran through the fallen foliage. One of Junior's responsibilities was raking leaves in the large back-yard of our family's home. My parents purchased the seven acres in 1975, just before I was born. Junior didn't have to rake it all, but along the tree line was a priority. At the end of his raking shift, even though he had to be ex-hausted from the extensive yard work, he would come in the house and res-cue me from the dullness of the country day.

Escape.

Once outside, I could see the vibrancy of the trees. Reds, oranges, yel-lows, with hints of the most persistent green captured the eye gate in every direction. The sun slightly peaked through, landing on the fruit of Junior's labor, spotlighting the symmetry of his work. Meticulous. Junior's efforts had resulted in a few average piles of leaves, gathered in semicircular heaps near my swing-set. Gargantuan mountains of opportunity to me, as Junior recruited me to take the leap to attempt to discover what existed beneath the surface of the mounds of fallen soldiers. I dove into the colorful darkness. Buried under the dead leaves in a wonderland of hidden existence. Junior brought the family's polaroid outside to instantly immortalize the moment.

Me, with a mini-fro, nicely rounded like the piles of Junior's leaves. Somewhat warmed by an unbuttoned, Detroit Lions jacket (I was never a Lions fan. Cowboys forever. But, I liked Billy Sims; I could not deny Billy Sims). Levi's blue jeans, flaring out a tad at the bottom. High-top, black Con-verse All-Stars with white laces tied tight. The pictures showed joy, excite-ment, and love. The real source of my warmth stood behind the camera. Junior's enjoyment was watching and capturing my enjoyment. No doubt he would have to regather the leaves after my escapade, but he didn't mind. To him, it was worth it to see me peak my head through the leaves as he seized the moment in which I seized the day. How wonderful it was to be sur-rounded by someone who just wanted to see me happy.

That was not uncommon for Junior. He often thought of ways to make me smile. Many times by driving me in his big, old, green Mercury Cougar to pick up my buddies: Brent, Adam, and Mike, and take us on some excur-sion. It didn't matter that we'd smell the fumes and couldn't hear one another's expressions of joy because of the lack of a proper muffler. We just talked louder, wiped our fume-infested, watery eyes, and sat ready for the next stop.

Even after he moved away, I looked forward to Junior's visits home. He would focus on me. During the trip, he'd surely offer me some made-up challenge, leading to the guaranteed ownership of some giant chocolate bar, massive sugar daddy, or enormous colorful, whirly sucker. *Hop on one leg while you hold your breath for twenty seconds, and I'll give you the candy*, full well knowing he had purchased the candy for me in the first place.

As a young adult, he lived in Kalamazoo, Michigan. Each summer I was permitted to spend two or three weeks in Kalamazoo, usually one of those weeks with Junior and the rest of the time with Stephanie, who had also landed there.

Kalamazoo was much different than White Cloud. There, for the first time, I had mostly black friends. I would ride bikes with peers whose real names I still don't know. People who were identified as Biscuits, Two, and Pumpkin. We rode our bikes all over the North Side of Kalamazoo. Houses next to houses, unlike what I was accustomed to in White Cloud. In Kalamazoo, you could hear the sounds of the neighbors. Their music, their televisions, their arguments, their laughter. It all pushed through their walls, infiltrating   ours.

In late-80's White Cloud it had become somewhat irregular to see a black person. On the North Side of Kalamazoo, it was rare to see a white person. It was there I was first informed that I "talked white." I later discovered that meant I spoke proper English—apparently too proper. I relaxed it there to better fit in. I learned what a candy store in somebody's house was. I learned what made little black girls my age laugh. I learned that there was an entirely different way of life for black kids in Kalamazoo than for black kids in White Cloud. In White Cloud, as a black boy, I was alone. In Kalamazoo, as a black boy, I was one of many. No one was surprised to see me. Grown-ups didn't tell me to call them by their first names. Everybody ate dinner, not supper. There was a shared experience. A shared culture.

I always looked forward to the week I would spend with Junior. When it was my time to stay with him, I knew I would feel free. On Junior's week, he would try to give me whatever I wanted. It was like he understood that I had been boxed in. He knew what it was to be boxed in. You want candy?

Okay. You want television? Okay. What do you want for dinner? Junior was an amazing cook, so the food options were stellar. Anything from home-made pizza, to delicious lasagna, to creatively plated fruit spreads in the shape of faces and such. It was like living a week with a kids' menu.

His house was meticulously clean and comfortable, always with some sort of unique furniture. He loved furniture probably more than he loved cooking. Incense burning, Patty Labelle playing in the background, an invit-ing sofa and fancy end tables, perfectly placed. Modern art on the walls with just the right balance of coordination and contrast. Black art. Unique visu-als. Modern pieces. I remember a picture of a fierce lion that made me feel like I was in the home of a king. This man had taste.

The week was about me and me only. Junior liked taking me out to breakfast. His restaurant of choice in downtown Kalamazoo, *Theo & Stacy's*. He would later recount the story of how every time he would take eleven-year-old me there, I would order steak and eggs and a large glass of orange juice, not realizing that I was challenging his budget. He never complained. He didn't stop taking me. I knew no better. Junior was my big brother. He'd do anything for me.

When I graduated from high school, I went to Grand Valley State Uni-versity in Allendale, Michigan. Junior lived about twenty minutes away in a small rental house in Grand Rapids, near the corner of Grandville Avenue and Franklin Street. At that point, my friends and I would frequently visit Junior's house. Jevon, my friend/brother who grew up with me in the church, and Damyon, my cousin from California who had recently moved to Michigan. We would go to Junior's banking on the enjoyment of his latest culinary masterpiece. At that particular time, it was often fried green toma-toes or authentic orange chicken, crab rangoon, and fried rice. We would play spades and dominoes, and we'd always find something to laugh about.

I later transferred to Ferris State University in Big Rapids, Michigan and not long after Junior found himself living there too. He was working on making some changes in his life. He briefly got married to an old friend from his childhood days at church. He renewed his membership at the White Cloud Church of God in Christ. No longer did he want to be em-ployed. He wanted to be an employer. He pulled together some money he had been able to save, and from some family members who were willing to contribute, and he used his resources to open his own restaurant called *The*

Soul Spot. It showcased his highly developed culinary skills. Mostly evolved from trial and error at job after job. Experience laid on top of his brief, formal, culinary training. I was so proud of my big bro.

I even worked for him on grill duty, prepping and grilling his tantalizing meat. Outside, in front of the storefront building you would find me creating the smoke and aroma that would serve as the principal advertising, wooing customers to give the new restaurant a shot. He taught me how to effectively and consistently barbecue. Seasoning with just the right hints of onion and garlic powder, seasoned salt, and pepper, along with a couple secret ingredients that I'll keep in the family. Massaging the rub into the rack of ribs, and placing on the grill with charcoal blazing at a steady smolder. I still hear his voice when I grill. Don't let it dry out.

I exited the highway in the heart of Nashville. Not far from TSU now, the rest of my commute was on city streets. Meandering through the hood, I smelled the smoke of similar soul spots heating up their grills in advertisement and preparation for the day's lunch rush. I couldn't help but wonder if they could compare to Junior's flavorful spread of perfection. I had watched people flock to the restaurant for his mouth-watering ribs and chicken, delectable greens and macaroni and cheese, and his famous caramel cake. That cake would hit your mouth causing you to have a taste experience like none other. The perfect caramelization—decadence meets baking mastery—leading to an indulgence that would repeatedly bring about attempted repentance, followed by the addition of unwanted pounds. I was sure God understood.

I would advance through life. Get married. Finish college. Begin my career. Start a church. Have a baby. Move to Tennessee. One thing I could always count on was that wherever Junior was, he was proud of me. He would say things like…"Aw, that's my little brother. I love my little brother." He would tell me that he thought I was *good* and couldn't do any wrong. He believed that. He was obviously wrong. But, he believed that.

Approaching my office, I hit a red light. The last stop before my final turn. The gas station on my left was busier than I would have expected at that early hour. The area is home to many people with no home. At 7:20 a.m., the pedestrian crossing in front of me was engaging in a liquid breakfast, the forty-ounce kind. More thoughts of my big bro. Junior had been homeless from time to time. Throughout much of the time described above, he struggled with alcoholism. I don't think I ever heard him say it, but I believe he always knew that he was an alcoholic.

For most of the last two decades, during visits with Junior, the stench of his everyday cheap whiskey permeated him. Five Star whiskey, mixed with whatever beer was at his disposal, usually a forty ounce of malt liquor—the reek of it oozed from his pores. He would prepare for his interactions with family members by pre-treating himself with this coping medicine, knowing that most of us weren't the crowd that would engage with his pastime.

I remember during one of those Kalamazoo visits while I was staying with my sister, Stephanie, Junior came over so drunk that people apologized to me for his drunkenness. I was a little older then. Old enough to know that alcohol was not his friend. Wondering if he knew as well. When he drank he was louder, and sloppier. Sloppy, that day, not realizing appropriate social distancing. Less in control of what words stumbled out of his mouth. More normally off-limits words than usual, followed by apologies to me, as if I hadn't heard the words before. He always worked through it. Stuck with his habit of maintaining a job—the habit he had started in his teenage years. He became more and more private over the years. Isolated. Sometimes coming out of hiding. Sometimes remaining in. He didn't let me in, but I could only imagine those alone moments. His focus had to be on escaping, wishing to be released from struggle, stress, and from worrying about making ends meet. Drink. Black-out. Escape. Freedom. It wears off. Recovery. Awakening. Remembering. Sobering. Bound. More bound. Repeat. Repeat again.

Broken.
Painful.
Cycle.

That day, when I pulled through the guard's gate approaching my new office, I had reached the point where I didn't try to call him as much. I felt like my efforts weren't reciprocated. There were so many attempts to reach him where he wouldn't answer. My mind would recall how when I did catch him the conversations were often challenging. How elusive my baby's name was to him. I had to remind him each time I called, "Kayden, her name's Kayden," because the name always slipped his mind. I'd answer the same questions repeatedly on calls because he didn't remember the previous answers.

I remember countless times going to Junior's apartments and knocking on the door. I'd wait, feeling the eyes of his neighbors who undoubtedly had stories of encounters, sounds, and experiences with Junior while under the influence. I waited, knowing he was inside. He wouldn't answer the door. My guess is that sometimes he was passed out; other times, he didn't want to be seen. His homes weren't as organized anymore. He still liked unique furniture, but what used to be spotless, became stained. The lingering odor of stale liquor replaced the incense. The sight of empty bottles—it was no longer meticulous. It was no longer welcoming.

Junior worked strange shifts. He no longer had the restaurant, which he closed at the height of success. His brief marriage ended after several months. His business ended. His dreams seemed to end, too. Life was leading him back to Grand Rapids. Back to coping. Back to struggling. Back to employee. Back to cheap whiskey and malt liquor. Back to escaping. Back to the cycle. Back. He no longer even enjoyed cooking—said he forgot how to make the caramel cake. He was a factory worker trying to make ends meet, usually working third shift. My best chance to catch him would be at seven or eight in the morning. He'd answer, wide awake, sometimes slurring speech, always with the sound of ice rattling in a cup in the early hours of the morning. My early-morning, unrestrained sarcasm would inquire if he was drinking iced coffee. He would laugh and move the conversation forward. He would ask about our move, about Camille, always probing, in a requesting kind of way, "Is she pregnant?" with a slight laugh. "How's your daughter? What's her name?" Over time, the calls became less frequent. It was not uncommon to be unable to contact him. He was elusive. I internally knew he heard the ring, he saw the caller-ID. It took months of attempts to catch him.

He no longer had an apartment. He lived from motel to motel. Sometimes, from motel to shelter. He didn't want to impose his problems on us. He didn't want to ask for help. He didn't want to receive. He didn't want to need. He didn't want to bother. So, he didn't call as much. He didn't answer as much. And, on my first day of work, we hadn't talked in a month. I had tried to catch up with him during a recent trip to Michigan, but he didn't answer. He especially didn't answer if he knew I was in town. A lot of times, he didn't want to be seen.

He wanted to see me. He wanted to know my daughter's name. He wanted to play in the leaves with her. He wanted to know what was new in my life. He wanted to celebrate my new position. He wanted to laugh. He wanted to smile. But, life was different. He was different. His living situation was different. He didn't want to be seen. He had no desire to be caught in the polaroid he had used to capture my image in the leaves.

Walking into my new office, fully decorated with a fierce picture of a tiger on the wall, I was reminded of the lion picture in Junior's home. I wanted to share the joy of my new job with him. I wanted to play spades and dominoes, and visit like we did in times past. I wanted to take him out for steak and eggs to repay the nearly thirty-two year debt, but he didn't want to be seen. So much so that in the weeks leading up to my new job, no one could reach Junior. Usually, someone was aware of his location, but we couldn't find him.

That wasn't the first time Junior had been admitted to the hospital. My big brother wasn't exactly the picture of health. His way of life caused his blood pressure to constantly be at stroke levels. His way of life distanced him from those who loved him most. His way of life caused him to feel ashamed. Less than. Alone.

So, I started work trying to get my bearings at TSU. I had to get oriented. Get my staff ID. Set up my email. Learn the layout of the campus. Find my files. I was breezing through the day, excited about the impact I would make. The day was about half over when my cell phone rang: a call from Stephanie. She had been visiting with Junior in the hospital for a couple days once we found out that's where he was. He'd been there almost a week. Once Stephanie arrived, she had been keeping me updated on his progress. On that call, Stephanie had a somber sound to her voice, but was also calm. She told me that I might want to get up there as Junior wasn't doing very well. She really did sound calm. Was she acting calm or being calm? I wasn't sure. No time to investigate. I had to go, as I had a meeting coming up. I kept working. It was my first day of work. I'd just left Michigan. I'd just tried to check on him. *He'll be alright.*

Camille called me to see how work was going. I told her of the challenges I was facing. What I had figured out. What I was working on. In passing, I mentioned Stephanie's call about Junior. Camille always seems to feel something at just the right times. She feels, and I trust her feelings. She said, "We should go; you should make plans to go up there." Was I so focused on the new job that I missed the seriousness of what Stephanie was saying? Did I mistake her calmness for peace? Camille's response shook me back to reality. The reality that the most important people we have to see about are our loved ones.

I called my boss on day one of my new job, and I apologized, and explained that I needed to get to Grand Rapids and wouldn't be in for day two of my new assignment. I went home, attempted to rest, and received a few update calls from my family. Restless. At 4 a.m. Camille, Kayden, and I packed up the car and took off driving to Michigan to check on my big brother.

On the way, the calls became more frequent and more intense. "He's not doing well."

"Let me talk to him," my tone was slightly sharp.

"He can't really talk. The words aren't coming out. He can't talk. Just pray. You need to get here as quickly as you can, Razel."

Adrenaline. Worry. Anxiety. Fear. Yes, fear. The calmness in the updates was a fleeting memory. Replaced with panic. Melancholy. Void of hope. Through Tennessee, through about an hour of Kentucky. Another call: "Razel, where are you? Junior's asking for you."

What do you mean asking for me?" He wasn't the type to ask for anybody…He didn't want to be seen. The tears flowed and the speed further intensified. "Tell him I'll be there as quickly as possible."

I was burning highway. The car was quiet. None of the objections Camille would normally make about my speed. Kayden, with sensibilities beyond her years, made no requests for the extra stops that typically delay the speed of our trips. It was so quiet, all I could hear was my thoughts.

Consciously breaking the law through Kentucky. Indiana. Indiana felt longer than a state should be on this trip. Indiana. Indiana. Time seemed to sit still in Indiana. Have you ever had an intense song playing in the car while you're driving and found yourself going faster than you realized? Each call formed the pulse of metal in double-time. Snare snapping on the 1-2-3 and 4. Guitars blazing. I broke the law in order to be compliant with the direction given me. Hurry.

I wished I would've called more. I wished he would've answered more. I needed him to pull through this. *Why can't he talk? What do they mean, can't talk? If he can't talk, how was he asking for me?* Silence. My thoughts were interrupted every now and then by a soft question from Camille. "You alright?" The question loaded with concern. She was not used to seeing me struggle like this. Not like this.

My tears answered truthfully. My mouth tried to convince me and Camille of a different answer. I tried not to bring Camille and Kayden into my state of panic. "I'm alright. Just concerned." The truth? I wasn't alright, but I was practicing. I knew I needed to be strength for Camille and Kayden. I knew I would need to turn on strength for Theresa, for Stephanie, for Jerome. My mom. I knew she would be a wreck. Her baby. She was the force of unconditional love for her children. For Dad. This was his firstborn son. His namesake. I'm the youngest of the crew, but it was no secret that they looked to me for strength. The weight was piling on and I wasn't even there yet. To them, I reflected spiritual strength. Theresa was the trailblazer. Stephanie was the nurse. Jerome was the athlete. I was the pastor.

For Junior, I needed to get there to be strength for Junior. Either God would push him through this or pull him from this. Either way, Junior was about to take a journey.

I answered another call hoping for a better report. Without taking a chance of receiving bad news, I immediately began reporting my location. "Just hit Michigan about twenty minutes ago. Finally out of Indiana. I'll be there in about an hour."

It should've taken closer to two, but I made it just after the stated time. Arriving at the hospital, I was ushered into his hospital room. The situation was even worse than they had described. What I didn't know was that my name was the last comprehensible verbal utterance Junior was able to make. He pushed it out. He demanded it out. Through the tubes. Through the seizures. Through the impairment. "Where's Razel."

Stephanie confirmed. "Junior, did you say Razel?"

He exhaled and nodded in relative relief, before she explained. "He's on the way."

I arrived in the room. Junior was crying from the pressure of physical and emotional pain. Spiritual pain. My sisters were crying with pain of their own. My brother Jerome, sat in the waiting room, navigating the stress of the situation. He resisted entering the room at that time. He didn't want to see his childhood playmate, his lifelong fraternal companion, in this condition, but he had to be present. He was present. My father portrayed faith in the face of adversity. Faith regardless. My mother was full of strength—empty of strength. The situation was serious.

I immediately and instinctively knew that the reason he fought to speak my name, to express my name, through the pain medicine, through the slowed brain activity, through the weight of what was upon him, was because he desired for me to pray for him. I'm the pastor.

The first thing I did upon arrival was not cry. I did not comfort my family. I did not spend time speaking to medical staff. I prayed. I prayed for his healing briefly. That was my desire. It couldn't be the end. I disturbingly felt that was not the direction my prayer was supposed to continue. In that moment, I had the thought. The feeling. The clarity. The understanding to realize my desire wasn't where the situation was headed. I sensed that a better prayer was for his comfort. "Help him to know that he is alright with me," was the direction I felt God leading, so I told him of how he was loved by God. Despite habits. Despite choices. In spite of. Loved by God. Ultimately, I realized that the best prayer of all was for his eternal security. That's what he wanted me there to do. This was why he beckoned the pastor. His unspoken request was, "Lead me to where I'm supposed to be."

This was a heavy responsibility. A heavy load. I hoped I'd get it right. It was a matter of life and death. Eternal life. He believed in me. He was proud of me. He trusted me. He thought I was *good*—he thought I could do no wrong. I prayed.

Just about an hour after that prayer, Junior was no longer conscious.

Several hours later, Junior was no longer with us.

Escape.

The combination of alcohol, poor health, out-of-control blood pressure, poor resources, inconsistent insurance, inconsistent housing, epilepsy, strokes, and struggle. Fifty-four years of struggle led to Junior's departure from this world.

I was so glad I made it, so glad I could pray…so sad that was all I could do. I wanted to change the outcome. I wanted to reverse the situation. But, sometimes all you can do is pray.

The next time I went back to my office at TSU, I once again thought of Junior when I saw the picture of the tiger. I fought through reliving that challenging first day. I pushed through and focused on making changes at TSU, ensuring equity and inclusion for all—allowing myself to be distracted by my work.

Escape.

Resting Peace

DANIEL ABBOTT
GRAND RAPIDS, MICHIGAN 2020

Denny called me the night before Mom died. It was kind of late and he didn't start talking right away, which was weird. Denny almost always calls for a specific reason and almost always gets right to the point. That night there was silence between us before Denny broke it by saying he just wanted to check on me. There was something off about him. Something bizarre in his tone. Concern or worry. Like he'd had a premonition of my pending doom and was just calling to hear my voice, to confirm I was still alive.

We didn't talk for long. Denny told me he loved me before he hung up the phone. I told him I loved him in return. I lay there that night with my three-year-old son Jude tucked in the crook of my arm. I'd been sleeping in his bed with him for the past few weeks. Vanessa was pregnant with our second child, in her third trimester and she was uncomfortable in her skin. I wanted to give her more space to sleep in our bed.

The night before Mom died, I lay there for some time thinking about Denny's call. I held Jude a little closer that night. I listened to my heart beat with my hand over my chest. I breathed deep and exhaled slow, wondering if I would wake up the next day, imagining my son finding me dead. Denny had me shook. I'll admit it, I was scared.

When Vanessa and I were married on August 7th of 2015, Denny stood as my best man. My little big brother. He stood beside me, I imagine, with the pride a big brother would feel. He'd seen me at my lowest. Saw me limp out of my twenties wounded. Saw me strap up my boots in my thirties, accept responsibility for my failures, throw on my hardhat, and accept the responsibility of my destiny. The birthing process of my future. The pains that came with it. The uncertainty that came with it. He saw my fight. He saw me fight. He saw me prevail.

I moved out of his basement in the space between graduating from Grand Valley State University and attending graduate school at the Vermont College of Fine Arts. Shortly after matriculating at VCFA, I met Vanessa and got choke-slammed by God. Told, not by His words, but with a feeling in my chest: "Vanessa Lynne Gant is your wife." It was jarring and life-changing. It was terrifying. I didn't want a wife. Didn't even want a girlfriend. I'd made the choice to be alone until I finished grad school and published my first novel. Until my children were grown. A wife wasn't part of my plan. Vanessa Lynne Gant and God had other ideas.

Man makes plans and God laughs.

When Denny called me the next morning, I knew it was bad. I woke up that day feeling happy to be alive, still feeling the effects of his call the night before, still analyzing his tone, looking for clues, trying to crack the code of the strangeness I felt. Denny choked on his words when he told me Mom was gone. I'd known Denny almost thirty years and that was the first time I ever heard him cry. "Please, don't come over," he told me and then he hung up the phone.

I sat at the dining room table and tried to keep it together. Jude was sitting on the couch watching cartoons. "What's wrong, Dad?" he asked me, before the tears came. I moved into the kitchen, away from my three-year-old son. I didn't want to scare him. I buried my face in my hands and rested my elbows on the kitchen counter.

Stevie called a couple hours after Denny did. We hadn't spoken in years. He'd been living in Houston with his wife and three of his four children. Said he was catching a flight in a couple days and staying for the week leading up to the funeral, which gave me comfort. I knew Denny and I wouldn't be alone. I couldn't think of a better distraction than Stevie, who has a way of both being there for you and lightening the mood at the same time.

Razel called shortly after Stevie did. And what's crazy about my relationship with Razel is that we always seem to communicate on time. A word spoken in either direction sways a feeling. A conversation makes an emotion make sense. Something I cannot quite articulate is articulated through him. That day Razel confirmed something I'd been feeling. "Don't let too much time pass before you go check on him," he told me.

I gave Denny one day. The next morning I bought two gas-station coffees and pulled into his driveway. We'd gotten snow the night before. Michigan snow. More than a foot if I remember correctly. It was still coming down. Those heavy flakes that appear to float. That movie-still snow. The kind of flakes children like to catch on their tongues. My little Camry almost got stuck pulling into Denny's driveway.

When I knocked on his door, no one answered, so I called. The call went straight to voicemail. I beat on the door with the soft side of a closed fist. Nothing. I sat in my car for a while and sipped my coffee, imaging Denny comatose drunk, laying on his kitchen floor. I considered breaking down the door or the glass picture window overlooking the yard. I considered it, but my gut told me Denny was fine. That he just wasn't ready to talk.

I sipped my coffee. I didn't want the responsibility. The most difficult responsibility I'd ever been commissioned. I had to be strong for the strongest man I've ever known. I called him again and left a voicemail. Told him to call me when he was ready to talk. Told him I was there for him, whatever he needed. Then I got out of my car and did the only thing I could think of. I shoveled his driveway.

My first novel, *The Concrete* is dedicated to Denny. The inscription reads "This book is dedicated to my brother Dennis. For over twenty-five years of unwavering love and support." Twenty-five years. Unwavering. Love. Support.

I don't have many friends. Don't need them. Don't want them. One Denny is worth a battalion of friends. One Denny. Someone who has believed in me with words and actions. "You're the hardest worker I know, bro. But you weren't ever going to make it to the NBA. You weren't ever gonna make it as a rapper. That writing shit, though. That's your ticket. You got talent. That's something I know you can do."

Never underestimate the power of being believed in.

Who lets a single father of six move into his house basically rent free? How many people see you? The real you. When the rest of the world writes you off. Give me my brother. You can keep your friends.

Denny called me back later that day. He sounded good. He sounded strong. He laughed about me shoveling his driveway. He told me he wanted to spend the week leading up to the funeral around family and close friends. I told him I'd be there. Whatever he needed. Shortly after speaking with him I texted Razel and told him Denny sounded like himself. Raz and his family would be arriving the day before the funeral. He would officiate the service and his wife, Vanessa's sister Camille, would honor the ceremony with a song. That gave me comfort. Made me feel a little less alone.

Kobe and Gianna died the same week as Mom and their deaths hit me hard. We had a dinner scheduled at Vanessa's brother, Ray's house for the day before the funeral. Razel, Camille, and Kayden met us there. It was the night of the Grammys. I sat on Ray's couch, appetite gone, drained, watching the Grammys pay tribute to Kobe's life. I held back tears. Both Mom and Denny were lifelong Laker fans. The loss of Mom was enough. Kobe and Gianna took me over the edge.

That night after we got Razel and his family settled into our apartment I made the drive over to Denny's. I don't remember much about that night. Who was there. What we talked about. I do remember talking about Kobe though. Denny told me, "God got a titan." He gave me his prophet look. Sometimes my brother speaks and it's like his words are coming from someplace else. That night he said, "Bro, you're a titan too. We all have a part to play in the next world. You're a titan, bro," he told me. "It's your heart. God always looks to a man's heart."

The next day on the way to the funeral I told Vanessa what Denny said and I lost it. I cried. Couldn't get the words out. I didn't feel like a titan. Didn't want to be a titan. I wanted to mourn. I knew my mourning would have to wait. I knew mourning is not what Denny needed, not from me. What he needed was me there, by his side, strong. I fought the emotions for a few moments and I finally told my wife, "I have to keep it together today. I have to be strong for my brother. I don't know how I'm going to make it, but I have to."

When we parked at the church in Cedar Springs, Stevie was in the parking lot waiting for me. I love Stevie. I've never loved him more than in that moment. Vanessa had to drive to Newaygo to pick up my twin twelve-year-olds, Andi and Lauren, who had spent the previous night with my parents. She and the girls would meet me at the funeral later. I thought I would have to walk in alone. Stevie meant I wouldn't have to walk in alone.

I walked through the doors of the church and saw a mural of pictures. Denny was standing in front of it and our eyes met. I started to cry before he grabbed me. Not to comfort me, but to put me in check. "Don't," he whispered. "If you lose it, I'm going to lose it. Promise me, bro," he said. "Promise me you'll keep it together."

"I will," I said. Then I wiped my eyes. I got myself together. I owed him that. I owe him more than that. I owe him more than I can ever repay. Dennis Cartwright is pound for pound the strongest man I've ever known. An alien. I worry for my brother. George Floyd was not a weak man, he was a compliant man. He was still executed in broad daylight. Denny is not a compliant man. Ten racist cops could never get him to the ground. He would never die beneath a white man's knee. Would never stand by with his smartphone, recording another black man dying beneath a racist cop's knee. He'd speak up. Fight if he had to. A racist cop would have to shoot a man like Dennis Cartwright. And they would shoot him.

If you ask Denny, he will tell you: "I'm a patriot. I love my country." A country that doesn't love him back. Doesn't love him black. A patriot. Let that register. A black patriot. In a country that will not acknowledge that Black Lives Matter.

As the white adopted son of a black woman. The white adopted brother to her four black children. The husband to a black wife. The father of eight biracial children. I have had the privilege and horror of viewing racial inequality in America through an uncommonly intimate lens for a white person. For years I have witnessed inequality and I have chosen silence. For years my friends and family have asked me to use my voice, but I had always declined. I've always preferred to hide beneath a hoodie. To lean against the wall. To deal with racism within the confines of my shrinking circle of trusted humans.

I'd joke with my wife, my friends, and family that I was doing my part: I was making America a browner place. That I was sticking it to white supremacists one beautiful black child at a time. When Tamir Rice was murdered. When Treyvon Martin was murdered. Even when Ahmaud Arbery was murdered. I ignored that pit in my stomach and changed the channel. Clicked X. Scrolled down. I looked away.

I can no longer look away. White America: you can no longer look away.

When I witnessed the execution of George Floyd. When I saw the demonic expression on Derrick Chauven's face. I couldn't look away. The faces of my sons were beneath that knee. Kevin. Twenty. He has aspirations of being an architect. Kevin's a good man, but with a temper like his dad. Simeon. Nineteen. Reckless like I was at his age, but with a kind heart and a head full of dreams. My little ones, Jude, just three, and Jackie, not even three- months-old. My four sons have to grow up in this country. They have to grow up with brown skin in this country. They have to grow up as black men in America.

I can no longer look away. White America: you can no longer look away.

Our country has not evolved. We have allowed the senseless killings of black Americans to be a black problem. This is an American problem. This will continue to be an American problem until white people step out of their bubbles and acknowledge the racial inequality in our country. Stop denying. Stop saying All Lives Matter when you haven't taken the time to understand what the Black Lives Matter movement means. Stop. Just stop.

Enough is enough.

Let's make America great. Let's think about the word Great. What it means to be Great. What we can do to make America Great. There is nothing Great about systemic racism. There is nothing Great about racial inequality. There is nothing Great about white police officers becoming judge, jury, and executioner after taking an oath to protect and serve. There is nothing Great about racist cops not being held accountable for murdering black Americans in cold blood on video.

Let's make America great. We have not been Great, white people. We have chosen to live in our bubbles. White people have chosen to be angry in silence, at our dinner tables, in conversations with people we know and trust. Our black brothers and sisters, our fellow Americans, need allies. They scream and they are not heard. They protest for their basic human rights and they are called thugs. Our black brothers and sisters have been losing this fight alone. We have watched the innocent die. We have mourned them with silence.

Enough is enough.

Silence is neutrality. Choosing not to stand up. Choosing not to speak up. Choosing not to lock your white arms with the arms of your black brothers and sisters. Choosing not to use your talents, your voices, your plat-

forms to fight injustice, makes you part of the problem, not part of the solution. White power has bullied you into silence. White Americans, we need
to be better. I pray that we choose to be better. To use our privilege to em-
power rather than oppress.

I will do my part. My peace will rest. My peace will wait for justice. For
equality. I will speak. I will write. I will not deny the problem; I will acknowledge the problem. I will be an instrument for change. I will use my gifts. My
voice. I will no longer look away.

White America: you can no longer look away.

Since the executions of Ahmaud Arbery and George Floyd there has
been a loud white presence on social media. An influx of support for the
Black Lives Matter movement. A call for action against injustice. I have seen
this before. After Trayvon Martin and Tamir Rice. White people scream for
weeks and then their screams become echoes. Become white noise. Become
silence. The latest black murder becomes old news. Until the next black
murder happens again.

I'm calling for white longevity. White persistence. White commitment
to equality. This is no battle. This is a war. Make no mistake, this is a war. Do
something. Anything. Whatever is in your power to do. Razel and I didn't ask
to write this book. It was our responsibility to write this book. Our experiences and our platforms demanded it. We answered the call. Answer yours.
You have your own talents. Your own platforms. There is something you can
do. I tell stories. I'm telling my story. The story of a white boy who grew up
in a black home. The story of a white man who loves black people. A white
man who worries for his black children. A white man who is tired of seeing
black people murdered by the police. By white racists. By White America.
We're better than this. God, I pray we're better than this. Let's make America
great. Let's lick our wounds. Let's be better than we've been.

There I was. A white man at a black funeral. Surrounded by family and
friends. Surrounded by people who have loved me and I have loved in return. People I call auntie and unc and cousin. People I call brother and sister.
On that, the worst day of my life, I belonged.

I didn't sit down at Mom's funeral. I stood in the back and Stevie stood
with me. We listened to Camille sing "Reckless Love." A song about the persistence of God. A song about unconditional love. Camille had been my

sister-in-law almost five years and I'd never heard her sing. "Before I spoke a word, You were singing over me. You have been so, so good to me. Before I took a breath, You breathed Your life in me, You have been so, so kind to me." Camille's voice gave me chills. I closed my eyes. I put my hand on Stevie's shoulder and I wept, but I kept my promise to Denny. I kept it together. My wife's sister has a beautiful voice. I'll never forget how she honored Mom. Then Denny spoke. Nothing watered down. He kept it real. My brother always keeps it real. Is the epitome of keeping it real. Razel took over. He was Raz. He was Pastor Jones. He was both. He riffed. People laughed. He spoke the truth. People wiped their eyes. Razel set the tone.

The microphone was passed around. People spoke of their experiences with Mom. My twenty-two-year-old daughter, Keyaira raised her hand. She stood. I moved past Stevie and up the aisle. Stood beside my oldest baby. She was so brave. She is so brave. She spoke about Grandma Diane. About unconditional love. She spoke of how she and her siblings, my children, were always treated like family. She spoke of those years in Denny's basement. She spoke on behalf of herself and her siblings. That's how she worded it. On behalf of herself and her siblings. A leader. My baby is a leader. I stood by her side. I've been proud of Keyaira countless times. I don't know that I've been prouder of her than I was in that moment.

We laid Mom to rest that day, but her legacy lives on. Through her children. Through her grandchildren. Through my children. Through all of us knuckleheads she loved, allowed into her home. Diane Cartwright never had much, but she always gave us everything she ever had. The most selfless human being who ever left footprints. That's who she was.

She will be missed. She is missed.

God, I miss her. I will continue to miss her.

Until I meet her again.

The Anonymous Poster

RAZEL JONES
SPRING HILL, TENNESSEE 2020

In the weeks following my brother's death, we mourned. We grieved. Junior was the first immediate family member we'd lost. We hurt. We cried. We remembered. We were comforted by the words of loved ones and friends. Even by the words of people we didn't know, but knew Junior. It was uplifting to know that he had touched peoples' lives for the better. He had been elusive with us. We didn't know what he was doing a lot of the time. But, the condolences of strangers filled in some of the gaps. They let us in on more of his story.

As people reflected on his life, I learned of how he helped coworkers get through the stress of their days with wise perspective and a realization that there was life beyond the job. How he would see a familiar face on the city bus and offer a smile to brighten their day. How he was willing to fearlessly fight to protect his true friends. How he bragged about me to people I didn't really know. How proud he was of my accomplishments. Confirmations of his belief that I could do no wrong.

In the months that came after his death, we experienced more death. More loss. More pain. We lost our community mom, Diane Cartwright. My godmother, Lera Jackson. Then, Covid-19 took the lives of over a hundred-and-fifty thousand people, including my pastor, our church leader in White Cloud, Bishop Robert Smith, Sr. Then, from one pandemic to another, we began to see a series of unnecessary, racially-motivated murders, starting with Mr. Ahmaud Arbery. More deaths—more pain.

In some ways I could relate to the family of Mr. Arbery. In some ways I couldn't. Mr. Arbery was out for a jog. Mr. Arbery stopped and looked at the construction of a house being built in his neighborhood. Mr. Arbery was murdered by two white men. Citizens. Not the owners of the house being framed and built. Not the police. Neighbors murdered him based on a suspicion that he'd done something wrong. There was no arrest, no trial, no jury, no verdict, and no appeal—just an execution. Execution for the crime of being black in their neighborhood. In his neighborhood. Racial violence. Racial murder. First degree privilege. Happening so often. Serial privilege.

The morning I looked up the dates of birth and death for Mr. Arbery, I stumbled upon his obituary on the Chavous B. Johnson and Reid Funeral Home's website. They handled his final services and remains. As I read the comments on Mr. Arbery's tribute page, I thought of when my brother died. I thought about the honor I had to be asked to deliver the eulogy for Mom Cartwright. I tried to use my words to comfort my friends. My family. My community. I thought of when I officiated my godmother's celebration of life. With everything in me, even though I was hurting, I desired to provide comfort to my godfather. My god-brothers. My family. My community. I thought about how Covid-19 hadn't allowed us to gather to have the type of celebration merited by the life of my pastor, but how we were still able to share stories, engage memories, and offer encouragement to his sons and wife. My family. My community. I recalled the comfort our families felt when kind words were shared about our deceased loved ones. This helped us smile through the pain. It was the love we felt, the funny memories shared, the stories of how our loved ones had contributed to other people's joy—those factors helped begin the ongoing process of healing. The words didn't take the pain totally away, but those words helped us. They helped me.

I wept for Mr. Arbery and his family and friends as I read comments from cowardly and anonymous posters writing statements on his tribute wall like, "…shouldn't have been stealing…" on a page for his family and friends to memorialize him. Paralysis…that was the likely intent of the heartless comments, and unfortunately their mission was accomplished. I couldn't move, all I could do was think. Mr. Arbery's family was robbed of their loved one and then robbed of the comfort the tribute wall was designed to provide.

Why would one feel the need or the liberty to trespass on such a space to spew the venom of judgement on this dead man and his living, grieving family? There is only one reason I can imagine…hate—the kind of hate that causes irrational actions for no defined purpose; the kind of hate that causes one to ignore human feelings and cross over reasonable social boundaries to attack the legacy of an individual and disrupt the healing process of human beings that you likely don't even know. This is hate based on skin color and melanin counts. Hate based on ignorance and fear of the unknown. Hate based on inaccurate and inappropriate feelings. Feelings of domination. Superiority. Supremacy. Feelings that still exist in our country. Our country.

The comments didn't stop there. The next posted by a hateful assumed name, F*#! Jogger, sarcastically stated, "His passionate drive to learn about architecture and jogging in basketball shoes led him to an early demise. Rip Jogger..."

Followed by another from assumed name, Nick Gurr—say it aloud and you'll notice that it's a play on that detestable slur created by slave owners, which was passed down through generational curses—generational ignorance—and continues to invoke anger and communicate hate. Nick Gurr's tribute reads, "Good night sweet prince, may you jog forever in heaven's housing developments. #BlackLivesMatter..."

Then, the next..."Jog on King. You were a good boy who didn't do nothing. R.I.P. in peas..." Don't miss the intentional use of the double negative, which comes back again in a later comment..."He was a good boy; He didn't do nothing..." first of all, applying the downgrading term, "boy," to this twenty-five-year-old man, just as slave owners and the generations that followed have addressed black men in times past. Further, through the double-negative, implying that Mr. Arbery did indeed do something to deserve his death, and using mocking language implying that Mr. Arbery's mourners, and all black people speak like slaves, our ancestors who were denied education and did the best they could to learn and apply a language that was not their native tongue. Finally, don't excuse the "rest in peas"—as this hateful individual and individuals of his/her kind willfully acknowledged their lack of desire for Mr. Arbery, Mr. Arbery's family and friends, and black people, in general, to have peace, instead wishing them to lay in the foul malodorous stench of peas.

Yet others, in-between many positive expressions of sympathy, empathy, and hope, posted fictionalized stories of made-up actions and scenarios they described as participating in with Mr. Arbery, involving theft, drugs, trespassing, and the like...Another stating his guilt, while yet another states, "He's jogging through construction sites in heaven..." Many of these comments are veiled, with intentions not easily understood at first read or first glance, similar to the operation of systemic racism and hate, covered with micro-aggressions, and defenses like, I didn't mean it that way, and You should stop playing the race-card. This veiled monster inhabits the daily life of the person of color.

Mind you, that hate—those comments—were posted on the site intended to bring comfort, peace, and healing to a family and friends mourning the loss of their son, brother, uncle, nephew, and friend. There were more comments, but I finally had to close the page after emailing the funeral home requesting that they please pull down the hurtful, ridiculous comments. I cried. I vented to Daniel. I vented to Camille. I laid on her shoulder, and I cried. Then, I wrote.

That personal, intimate space was invaded with vicious, hurtful words by heartless, racist people who felt entitled to speak, to joke, to mock, and to degrade this man and his loved ones. I believe the anonymous posters treated Mr. Arbery and his family as products of that ancient, constitutional belief that they were 3/5 human.

As I read the comments I quickly realized it was time for me to begin that everyday work necessary for a black person. To keep going to work. To the store. To the school. To continue functioning in a white world. I knew that I had to do the work of not doing what many white people have done to me. I had to calm myself, separate myself, and combat the thoughts that lured me to the simple, yet ignorant reaction of judging all white people, based on the heinous actions of some. Hating all white people. Blaming all white people. Excluding all white people. Once again, I could not allow the actions of some to defile my view of all.

How I wish everyone would do that work...stop seeing me as the stereotypical image you've come across in the media, or the one individual who wronged you. Just because one committed a wrong, does not mean that all are guilty. It is this lumping, this grouping, this stereotyping that simple minds use as a shortcut, instead of building meaningful relationships. Rather than pressing past the tendency to assume the next will be just like the last, simple-minded people limit their exposure to new experiences because of the negativity entangled in the previous experience. If you do that, you are the one missing out. If I do that, I am the one missing out. Missing out on the richness of connection to people with different experiences, knowledge, personalities, and practices—shoving myself into a box of broken mirrors, where my life is consumed with experiencing people who look, act, feel, and live, in a sadly, generic way, just like me. The broken mirror produces cuts. Gashes. Fragmented reflections of one's self. Wounds.

These commenters didn't consider Mr. Arbery human. They didn't consider his friends and family human. And, this is the reality and the context that people of color have to face and live within. The anonymous posters are our distanced neighbors, our distrusting coworkers, our detached classmates.

We are left to wonder…Is the anonymous poster the white guy I pass by in the grocery store who does not acknowledge my presence, looking like he hopes I don't engage him? Is the anonymous poster the white supervisor who keeps overlooking me for the assignment—the promotion—the responsibility? Is the anonymous poster the business owner who follows me around the store expecting that I'm going to steal the products that I plan to purchase? Is the anonymous poster the teacher who seems to keep giving me a hard time and poor review in the classroom while condoning the actions of the white students who are clearly not performing well? Is the anonymous poster the government official who calls brown and black protestors thugs and criminals, threatening to shoot them, while referring to white protestors as good people, even when they are white nationalists in Charlottesville carrying tiki torches to emulate the historic (and current) burning torches of the KKK, or carrying AK-47s and AR-15s to the state capital building in Michigan to voice disgust with a woman in power?

Who is the anonymous poster?

…Is it you?

Afterword

RAZEL JONES

It is my hope—our hope—that the stories Daniel and I have shared will make you think, and cause you to consider your own actions and your own stories.

To the white reader, we ask that you do the work to be part of the solution. To recognize that you have been given advantages that others don't have. That is not your fault, but it is your opportunity. It is your opportunity to use your influence to ensure equity for all. Use your inherited advantages as platforms to speak against injustice—to live against injustice.

To the black reader, the brown reader, the marginalized reader, we hope you find strength in recognizing that our normal is abnormal. You are not crazy. You are not wrong. Your experience is valid. Your frustration is valid. Your pain is genuine. Your wounds are real. Don't give up on healing. Don't give up on dreaming. Don't give up on thriving. Do the work to make sure we don't become what we hate. When you rise to a position of power—and we will rise—don't repeat the ignorance we've seen, we've felt, and we've experienced. Do better. Be better.

Together. Together is the only way we will truly overcome. Warriors and allies fighting together to destroy and rebuild our broken systems. War produces casualties. This war has produced far too many casualties. It is up to each of us to not allow those casualties to be in vain. Do not allow our wounds to be in vain.

Acknowledgements

First and foremost, we would like to thank God for planting the seed for this book and providing the fertilizer. From the onset we have felt empowered and purposed and have felt His presence every step of the way. It is our honor to share our experiences, explore the adversities we have conquered on our journey, and it is our sincere hope that this book contributes to positive change in the world.

We would like to thank Summer Camp Publishing for believing in our project and their willingness to push it along faster than what is customary in the publishing industry. Brooks Rexroat and Ali Braenovich believed in our vision, the urgency of the material, and delivered our book into the world at a frenzied pace without sacrificing the quality of our product. For that we are grateful.

We would also like to thank Camille Jones for her editorial contribution to the project. Her keen set of eyes were invaluable and helped push *Wounds* toward completion. And our last-minute readers, Carly Abbott, Jesse Davila, Mwenda Ntarangwi, Carla Roberts, and Jevon Willis. We are grateful for your support, your honesty, and your attention to detail. We appreciate you.

Though this is a work of creative nonfiction, we acknowledge that when dealing with memory, some memories almost forty-years old and beyond, there is no perfect truth. We have done everything in our ability to depict the situations in this book honestly, and have reached out to many people who shared these experiences with us to get the most accurate truth possible. We would like to thank Kevin A. Abbott, Keyaira Abbott, Savanna Abbott, Simeon Abbott, Sue Abbott, Dennis Cartwright, Kandis Cartwright, Stephanie Charles, Karen Cooley-Gordon, Brent Foondle, Camille Jones, Hendrick Jones, Sr., Jerome "Uncle Jerome" Jones, Jerome Jones, Laurel Jones, Paula Jones, Theresa Jones, Michael Sears, Suzette Shelmon-Murchison, Steve Thomas, Karen Thorington, Tracey Wicks, Karl Williams, and Jevon Willis for helping us fill memory gaps, add details, and fill in blanks. Your contribution to this project has been invaluable.

Razel Jones Thanks:

Daniel Abbott: You have awakened the creative writer in me. It's an honor to work with, and try to keep up with, such a gifted author. Friend. Brother. A definite ally in the struggle toward racial equity.

My wife Camille: You put up with me using every available moment to craft this book. My sounding board. As always, you empowered me to do better—be better. Thank you for your consistency. You keep everything together while I tear everything up. I don't want to imagine the mess I'd be without you. You are more than I bargained for (in a good way). I love you.

My gift, Kayden: When God gave you to us we knew we had just received the greatest gift of our lives. I know Uncle Dee and I have been spending a lot of time working on this book, but I hope one day you realize that you are my inspiration. I long for this world to be better for you than it has been for the generations that have come before you. There is a passion in you for justice. Your voice will inspire a generation. Keep thinking. Keep reading. Keep writing. The world needs you. I love you to the moon, the stars, the sun, heaven and back, twelve trillion times more than any number you can come up with.

The mighty, mighty Joneses: Mom and Dad, you are incredible. Thank you both, and Uncle Jerome for providing so much amazing information for me during this process. It has not and will not go to waste. You are phenomenal parents and people. I'm deeply blessed to have you as guides on this journey of life. Mom, Dad, Theresa, Stephanie, Jerome. All of us have had a tough time over the last year and a few months. No one is allowed to die anytime soon. I miss Junior; I know we all miss Junior. Yet, together we are Jones strong. Thank you each for blazing trails for me. Now, to all of our offspring: Stand on our shoulders. Go further. Achieve greater. Accomplish more.

White Cloud. You challenged me. You wounded me. You prepared me. My friends who journeyed with me, too many to list: Antonio, Jemar, Jevon, Brent, Mike, Bill, Adam, Deanna, Crystal, Angie…way too many to list…every friend from The Cloud. Thank you for being a part of my story.

Daniel Abbott Thanks:

Razel Jones: Raz, what a ride! It has been such an honor working on this project with you. I've never had this much fun writing and editing. The back and forth was amazing and being able to share the experience of bringing this book to life is something I will never forget. Cheers (Lifts Detroit Lions water bottle. Sips.)

My wife Vanessa: My dear wife, the unrealistic expectations you place on me push me beyond my limitations. You drive me absolutely bonkers, but you make me better, give me balance, and hold me accountable. Your refusal to accept less than my best makes me a better man. I love you so much.

My children: Keyaira, Kevin, Simeon, Van, Andi, Lauren, Jude, and Jackie, you are my joy. The oldest four, we've been through it. I cannot take back the basements, the struggle, or the poverty. The truth is, I wouldn't. My hope is that you remember the struggle. Remember my refusal to quit. I hope you allow your own childhood experiences to make you strong. The younger four of you are growing up with a different version of me. The me that has overcome adversity. The calmer me. The conquering me. I love all eight of my babies fiercely and uniquely. I'm proud of you all. And I'm so excited to see each of your purposes revealed and your stars ascend.

Mom and Dad Abbott: I know I was a challenge growing up. I know I softened you for my younger siblings. But I thank you for instilling in me my work ethic and my open-mindedness. You are both beautiful human beings. I am honored to call myself your son.

The Cartwright family: Crystal, Latrice, Denny, and Kandi, I mourned the loss of Mom with you and I will continue to mourn. Your family took me in and accepted me as your own. This book could not have been written without you. I could not have raised, could not raise biracial children without the unconditional love that Mom, that all of you have given me over the years. Being part of your family has opened my eyes. I love you all like my own. You are my own. I hope this book honors Mom. I miss her. God, I miss her.

Jesse Davila and Garrett Dennert: my friends. My writer friends. I value your willingness to always talk shop, provide a second set of eyes, and your support both professionally and personally. I value your friendship. I hope you both know that you have my love and support and that I will always be a champion for your work, your life's endeavors.

My mentors: Connie May Fowler, Caitlin Horrocks, Ellen Lesser, and Sean Prentiss, your enthusiasm and support for my work over the years has given me the confidence to navigate this crazy life as a writer. I am surviving this world because of your guidance. You are my roots.

About the Authors

 Razel Jones is a Diversity and Inclusion professional, speaker, and the Director of Equity and Inclusion at Tennessee State University. In 2016, he released his first book, *See What You Hear*, a piece about actualizing vision. Jones has a Bachelor of Arts Degree in English Language and Literature from Grand Valley State University and an Master's in Business Administration from Northwood University. He has professional certifications in Cultural Intelligence, HR, Strengths, Civil Rights, and Affirmative Action. He and his family reside in the Greater Nashville, Tennessee area.

Daniel Abbott is the author of *The Concrete* (Ig Publishing 2018). He has a Bachelor of Arts Degree in Writing from Grand Valley State University and a Master of Fine Arts Degree in fiction writing from the Vermont College of Fine Arts. His writing has appeared in pubications including Lit Hub, the Noctua Review, the Ginosko Literary Journal, and the Owen Wister Review. He lives with his family in Grand Rapids, Michigan.

CPSIA information can be obtained
at www.ICGtesting.com
Printed in the USA
LVHW022351310821
696547LV00007B/516